PASSED

12 PROVEN SECRETS TO PASS ANY PROFESSIONAL EXAM AT THE FIRST SITTING

PASSED

12 PROVEN SECRETS TO PASS ANY PROFESSIONAL EXAM AT THE FIRST SITTING

Ebrima B Sawaneh, FCCA

FULLADU PUBLISHERS
Kanifing

DEDICATION

This book is dedicated to my sweetheart Ndey Amie Sawo. September 2017 marks the 10th year of our marriage. Thank you for all the love and care. It is also extended to our daughter Kumba, who was the first proofreader of this book. I have not forgotten our son Kebba and his "Paw Patrol" team.

It is also dedicated to my parents Adama Fatty and Alhagie Bunja Sawaneh for giving me the opportunity to attend classes while they worked at the farm for the family's livelihood.

You guys gave me the opportunity and confidence to write this book. You also offered me support throughout the entire process.

Thanks for your support.

TABLE OF CONTENTS

ACKNOWLEDGMENTS

So many awesome people inspired me to write this book and helped make it better. All those who asked me questions about how to pass professional courses. Over 200 Facebook fans who signed on to become accountability partners of this project.

Young people around the world, all the members of the Self-Publishing School, the staff at Happy Self-Publishing, and my group study members from Nusrat High School to the Edinburgh Business School.

Thank you all for the support.

DOWNLOAD THE BONUS EBOOK

Don't turn another page without downloading the free **eBook: Tools for Productive Students**

http://ebrimasawaneh.com/passedgift

INTRODUCTION

There have never been more opportunities to become an expert in any field of life than there are today. It is not about your background, wealth, age or location. A few decades ago becoming a professional accountant, engineer, lawyer, etc. required wealth or influence as only a few people had access to classrooms, books, and money. Today, you have blogs, online courses, distant learning schools, and books that can support anyone to succeed in a professional exam.

In this book, I am going to show you some of the techniques used by students who have achieved success in multiple professional examinations. The book has been designed to help you plan for your studies and examinations; even without attending lectures. This book is for people who have the desire to be professionally certified but face challenges with time management, studies, note preparation, and the examination hall.

The book will not only guide you to pass exams but give you some common pitfalls that cause many students to fail their exams. It also offers some tips that would be useful; even beyond the examination hall.

As a lifetime self-study student who sat and passed over 20 professional exam papers at the first attempt, I have mastered the art of passing exams even while having a full-time banking job.

I have read, researched, and tested many of the best materials for success in any exam. I was able to pass the Certified Accounting Technician (CAT) and the Association of Chartered Certified Accountants (ACCA) within five years and without having to re-sit a single exam paper. This excludes the 10 MBA modules in which I graduated with distinction within a 2-year period.

Professional and academic students who struggle with their courses have already experienced success by implementing some of the tips and strategies found in this helpful how-to book.

Mamudu Jallow, a professional accounting student from The Gambia, said, "I could not have found a better one. These tips are essential for every student to read."

I promise, if you follow the strategies explained in this book, you'll get higher success rates in any exams compared to an average student. However, that is as far I can go. It is now up to you to apply these principles and achieve your desired outcome.

I know some professional associations permit students to continue re-sitting exams for more than five years, but you do not want to be the person who misses out on growth opportunities in life because you take too long to complete your professional qualifications. Be the kind of person other people would see and say, "I don't know how you were able to make it." Be the kind of person who acts and does so - immediately.

The exam tips and strategies you're about to read have been proven to create real results. All you need to do is keep reading and apply the concepts. Take control of your life right now, make it interesting, and enjoy the new life you're about to create with your new certification.

You have to read, think, and act; then you will see successful results.

As you go through this book and your studies, I want you to keep one important fact at the back of your mind. That the purpose of any professional exam is not just to secure a good job or clients but also to make you a better person. All professional training and certificates are a means to an end. You must continue to develop yourself and learn other values that will make you a better person.

Why this book?

Authors write books for many different reasons. However, mine is the result of the passion I have for helping and supporting other people who want to make a better living.

Following my successful completion of the accounting technician and professional qualifications through self-study, I have received one common question from colleagues and students. They asked, "How were you able to complete the ACCA programme within two and half years and without failing a single exam?"

In response to this question, I usually replied, "It was God, and I also studied very hard." However, people continue to ask the same question 5 years after the final exam, and some even requested mentorship. In June 2015, I decided to write an article about this on my blog (successvalues.com), and all the subsequent questions you may have are directed to this link.

The article trended and received multiple shares on social media, and in October 2015, I started to turn the article into a book with more information, including scientific findings.

Additionally, some people think it was just mere luck on my side to successfully pass all my exams. Nonetheless, you will later learn that my successes are based on what Brian Tracy (International Speaker & Bestseller) would call the Universal Law of Cause and Effect.

This law states that whatever output we achieve in life is a direct result of our actions in the past. To put it in another way, the effects we experience are directly related to causes. It is a principle that is observed in physics, religion, and personal success.

The burning desire to improve my conditions has also influenced me to study, practise, network, and sacrifice thousands of hours, and this also led to my exam successes.

I have also seen some students who dropped out of professional courses to pursue a degree programme as they felt that professional exams are too difficult to pass.

Furthermore, the exam pass rates for most professional associations have always been very low compared to the academic courses. For example:

- December 2016 - ACCA reported an average of a 58% pass rate for its fundamental level and less than 40% for the professional level. March 2017 was worse, as some subjects had a 35% pass rate.

- June 2016- CFA Level I had 43%, Level II 46%, and Level III 54% pass rates.

- In 2015, CIMA had a 51% pass rate for their operational level case study, while the USA CPA reported a 50% rate for the same year.

- Similarly, the Society for Human Resource Management (SHRM) and the Board of Bar Examiners both reported a less than 60% pass rate in 2016 for first-time takers.

These reports confirm that most professional exams produce less than a 55% exam pass rate. The pass rate is even poor among first-time takers.

With these results, the expected question is: Is there any way to improve one's chances of success in these exams? Yes, and in this book, I will show you how to pass a professional examination and how to do it quickly even if you are working full-time. I will share practical methods that worked for me in five different qualifications, and for every other student who used them.

Think and act today, and you will succeed in any examination.

Book structure

The chapters follow each other and by reading them in sequential order, you'll understand an approach that will help you to prepare for your exams.

Section One (*On your mar*ks) presents information about mindset, investment, and learning methods. If you start with a positive mindset, make some investment, and choose a suitable learning method, then everything will be in order for the following section.

Section Two (*Get set*) is full of tips and strategies to help you to prepare for an exam. Learning about the exam structure, syllabus, note preparation, learning from others, and focusing strategies. It also covers careful usage of past exam questions.

Section Three (*The exam and beyond*) reveals the unwritten laws of the exam hall. It starts with the pre-exam principles and ends with the techniques of answering exam questions. You will also learn how to make examiners happy in Chapter 2 of this section.

The final (*Bonus*) chapter details the benefits of professional certification. It is important for new graduates who are considering other qualifications for their careers and personal development.

Final advice: Put your shoes on, tighten the strings and be on your marks!

PART 1

ON YOUR MARKS

Purposeful Prior Planning Prevents
Poor Performance

CHAPTER 1

START WITH THE RIGHT MINDSET

> "You can be anything you want to be, if only you believe with sufficient conviction and act in accordance with your faith; for whatever the mind can conceive and believe, the mind can achieve." —**Napoleon Hill, Author of the bestselling book Think and Grow Rich.**

If the above quote from Napoleon Hill does not motivate you to believe that you can achieve anything in life, then reflect on your goals again. This first chapter is about your desire, faith, and actions. Your mind and actions must have some prerequisites position before you move towards a particular goal.

You may have set a great goal of acquiring a professional certification. However, your chances of achieving this goal can be very slim if you do not believe in your ability to pass the exams. Lack of self-confidence has always been one of the primary reasons why most people cannot achieve their life dreams.

I am not in any way referring to a qualification or career someone forced you to follow, but rather the one that can lead you to your goals. If you are going to be successful in passing the professional exam you desire, you must believe that you can make it happen.

During my five years of teaching accounting and finance at local colleges in the Gambia, I observed that most students who failed courses, such as accounting, are usually the ones who already believed that they could never pass the course even before attending the lecture. They used to say, "Mr Sawaneh, this course is tough, and I don't think I will pass it."

This type of mindset sabotages your exam success even before you put a single word on paper. You will not be motivated to study or revise, as you will not enjoy it.

You must remove the limiting belief that you can't pass an exam. If you believe you can pass or you believe you cannot pass any paper, then you are right. However, you should always remember that your self-belief is a good indicator of what you can achieve for yourself.

"The winner, after careful preparation, is confident he will win the war before he wages battle. The losers, without preparation, engage the enemy first, hoping they will win the fight." **—Sun Tzu**

An average student thinks about the fear of examinations even before attending classes. They study only to pass and that it is why exam failure is a major disappointment for them. Sun Tzu would call them the *losers*.

If self-doubt and negative mindset have been affecting you, then the strategies explained in this chapter will definitely boost your confidence as you prepare for any examination.

Burning desire

First and the most important starting point is the intense desire to acquire that professional qualification. Nothing can stop you from achieving your goals if you have a strong burning desire to be qualified.

Your goal of becoming a member of a professional body will most likely be triggered by a desire to make certain changes in your life. My desire was to get a high-paying job and great responsibilities in the accounting profession. Though I started with Certified Accounting Technician (CAT), my ultimate target was to acquire the ACCA qualification. I wanted to be an accountant who could practise in any industry, with a good pay, respect in society, and possibly have the qualification to secure an international job.

These strong desires kept me, the timid, shy looking young man focused, along with many sleepless nights while still working. The good feedback is that as of the time of writing this book, I am working for a multi-billion dollar international financial institution based in Nigeria.

Think of the reasons why you want to qualify in your profession. If they are strong enough, then they should be your motivation to study, research, and practise.

Take action

A burning desire is important, but on its own, it is not sufficient. You must decide at the very beginning that you want to be a professional. You must act on that decision, and make every possible effort to do whatever it takes to become qualified in your profession.

Know your abilities

The lack of certain skills has led many people to doubt their abilities to pass some exams.

For example, because you are not good at calculations, you think that a professional finance qualification is a no-go area. This issue makes some people drop out of their courses even after starting them.

However, you can minimise such problems by assessing your abilities against the primary skill requirement of the qualification. For instance, a finance qualification, such as a CFA, may require you to understand basic statistics. If you lack such prerequisite knowledge, then go for that first. It will make you more confident.

The key strategy is to overcome your weakness through additional learning. Do not think it's too late to learn something new that will lead you to happiness.

Believe in yourself even after failing an exam

Failure and rejection are part of life, and the only time you have failed is when you stop trying. In an examination, there are two types of failures for most people: failing to score the official pass mark or inability to achieve the target score you set yourself. Either of these reasons can discourage students.

However, if assessed well, failure can make you better as it provides learning feedback. Do not let a few failures drag you down. Face them and deal with them. Yes, it is hard, but you should not allow them to change your path to achieving your goal.

I have a friend called Musa Suwa, and his experience stood out in the journey to professional qualification. He is a perfect example of where hard work and perseverance can lead to success. Musa started off his career in 2007 working as an operations officer in a commercial bank in the Gambia.

Determined to become a chartered accountant, Musa strived to achieve his ACCA qualification albeit the high workload he was faced with. This was a challenge but Musa, fuelled with the burning desire for succeeding, he was ready to face it. In the process, he failed a few exams and had to re-sit an exam paper a couple of times, but he never gave up. He knew what he wanted, and he was going to get it.

Every failed exam paper was a learning opportunity for him. Where did he go wrong? What can be done to improve his results? How can he improve his grades? He tried to understand his weak areas and work hard for improvement.

Musa has no breaking point. He is currently the budget and planning Manager of a regional bank in Africa, where he oversees over 30 counties with a balance sheet of more than $24 billion.

Musa's example has shown that failing a few exams does not make you a failure. Failure comes about when you quit. It all comes down to one thing, how bad do you want it and how far you are ready to go?

Listen to positive people

You should try by all means to avoid listening to people who share discouraging comments about the course or the examination. Such comments can increase the frequency of self-doubt for you, particularly if you value such people's opinion.

I want you to know that many people have had successes in areas where other people think they cannot succeed. For instance, Thomas Edison, the inventor of the light bulb, was withdrawn from school by his mother as she was advised by the teachers that he was 'addled.' The school concluded that he was not capable of learning anything. Today, Edison is considered one of the greatest inventors of all time.

Similar challenges of failure and rejection stories happened to Oprah Winfrey, Albert Einstein, and many other successful people.

You should listen more actively to people who inspire and encourage you to go after your dream.

It is better to be with someone who will share some practical cases, exam tips or any other information, and who can make you a better professional than a person who will explain how it is impossible to pass one course.

In fact, I would prefer to be alone.

Why?

When you add positive 3 to negative 2, it gives you only 1. Similarly, if you always listen to negative comments on a course, it affects your ability to think positively about such an activity.

Listening to negative messages is what I call a *negative addition*. You are adding something to your mind, but it will ultimately take something from you.

You should be positive

You can receive positive advice and loads of lectures. However, nothing will work if you have a negative mindset. Your self-limiting belief can hold you up for years, as it puts fear and other negative thoughts in your head. It can create the negative thoughts that made you believe that certain exams are not meant for you.

> *You can force a child to the school, but you cannot force him to learn.*
> **—Ebrima Sawaneh**

Whatever qualification you have decided to pursue, you must think about your success positively and avoid listening to the negative self-talks that would hold you back.

Through decades of research and studies, Carol Dweck, a renowned psychologist at Stanford University and author of *Mindset: The New Psychology of Success*, groups successful and talented people into two general categories of mindset: fixed and growth mindsets.

Fixed mindset people believe that their primary qualities, intelligence, talents, abilities, are just fixed traits. They have certain skills, and that's that. But growth mindset people believe that even basic talents and abilities can be developed over time through experience, learning, and so on. And these are the people who do not always worry about how smart they are, how they look, what a mistake means. They challenge themselves and grow.

Growth mindset students will focus on the process; the process that engages them to succeed in their studies. So, if you want to succeed in any professional qualification, think about how to get there instead of why you cannot achieve it.

In 2015, I decided to start a blog that would educate thousands of young Gambians about personal finance and small business. Then, I had no idea about website management let alone coding. Yet, I wanted to set up a website that would achieve this goal with minimal cost.

I researched the world of website registration, development, blogging platforms, promotion strategies, etc. Within five months, I registered my first blog without anyone's technical support and also saved myself thousands of dollars. With continuous practice and more reading, today I can register, instal, and maintain websites, and I can even perform basic website coding.

Having the right mindset is essential to successful thinking, acting, and passing any exam. I want you to decide that as from today you can pass any exam. Think about your reason for pursuing the qualification, reflect on where you are coming from, and think about how good it will be when you finally finish that professional qualification.

Seek the company of the right people

Do you ever wonder why some parents ask their kids to only hang out with certain kids? They expect good kids to associate with other good kids.

Therefore, besides every successful student, there is a good mentor, family, and associates. As a matter of fact, an associate does not have to be your best friend. They can be your school lecturer, qualified professional, or like-minded student. You just want to associate with those who share similar values, interests, and aspirations.

I had the opportunity to be associated with people of different ages and working backgrounds when studying. Throughout my professional studies, I lacked money, but I never lacked individuals who shared similar values of personal development.

These were like-minded people who were either studying the same course or were interested in my personal development. Some of these networking partners were attending lectures, and they shared notes and study materials with me.

Today, all of us have our professional qualifications.

Be ready to pay the price

Behind the story of every successful student, there is a story of study, practice, and sacrifice. They are willing to pay the price to win the prize. The cost price of learning includes investing more money in the course materials, time, or a willingness to move out of their comfort zone.

> *Pay the price now, and you will receive the prize when the results are out* **—Fela Durotoye.**

I used to study till late in the night, and sometimes, I woke up early in the morning to study. If most people knew how I worked to pass my examinations, they would not think I was just lucky.

Self-discipline

A study conducted by the University of Pennsylvania researchers, Angela L. Duckworth and Martin E.P. Seligman in 2005 concluded that self-discipline is a better predictor of academic success than even intelligence quotient (IQ). The study looked at a group of 164 eighth graders in the United States, and the results were:

> *"Highly self-disciplined adolescents outperformed their more impulsive peers on every academic-performance variable, including report-card grades, standardized achievement-test scores, admission to a competitive high school, and attendance. Self-discipline measured in the fall predicted more variance in each of these outcomes than did IQ, and unlike IQ, self-discipline predicted gains in academic performance over the school year."*

You must have the discipline to plan, study, revise, and practise over and over again - until you achieve mastery of the course material. There are no better shortcuts to pass any exam than developing self-discipline and self-awareness.

Determination

Finally, you must have the determination to persist in spite of any temporary setback, including exam failure, financial obstacles, or even any social issues you may experience.

In the year 2000, I started high school with a strong desire to improve my life situation, especially financial independence. I believed this could only be achieved with excellent results in the West African Senior School Certificate and winning a scholarship to the University of the Gambia.

I had no access to a private lesson teacher; my only hope was to read my class notes consistently. Although all my scholarship applications were unsuccessful, even with excellent results, the effort did, however, help me build the right habit of self-study. It also supported my studies beyond high school.

I lacked the finances to study for a university degree, and all my scholarship applications were rejected, but I never gave up. It was a determination that helped me pursue my dreams even with all the difficulties.

Remember that believing in yourself is a choice, and it is an attitude you develop over time. You must choose to believe that you can pass any exam and be positive about it. After all, you want to add that professional certification after your name for a reason. This reminds me of a well-known poem written by Walter D. Wintle, where he expresses a great truth about confidence:

If you think you are beaten, you are;
If you think you dare not, you don't
If you like to win, but you think you won't,
It is almost certain you won't.

If you think you'll lose you've lost;
For out of the world find
Success begins with a fellow's will –
It's all in the state of mind

If you think you are outclassed, you are
You've got to think high to rise.
You've got to be sure of yourself before
You can ever win a prize

Life's battles don't always go
To the stronger or faster man;
But soon or late the man who wins
Is the man who thinks he can

Summary and action plans

Acquiring a professional qualification is a means to an end. You cannot pass any exam without acting with a positive mindset, self-discipline, and a willingness to explore. Here are a few action plans to implement as you prepare for your professional studies.

- List at least one reason why you want to be qualified – burning desire

- List three action points that will help you pass the exams

- List at least two people whose association can support your journey

CHAPTER 2

INVEST TIME AND MONEY IN PASSING EXAMS

> *"Many students cannot pass their exams because they failed to sacrifice the minimum capital of time and money."* **—Ebrima Sawaneh**

It was August 2009 when the ACCA results were released. John opened his email early in the morning to check if he had passed or failed the June exam. To his dismay, he failed all the two papers he attempted. His eyes were red, his voice changed, and he did not even take his usual morning tea.

"ACCA is now very difficult; it seems they make people fail" whispered John while walking towards his boss.

"I didn't make it again," he told his boss. "I don't know how, but I studied these papers very well."

"Sorry about that news," his boss replied. "But are you sure that you prepared well enough? I observed that your friends in other departments stayed to study their notes after work and sometimes came at the weekend. It also appears that you do not invest in study materials. You always borrow from others, even though you can afford it. May I advise that you change your strategy and invest money and time in this course."

There is a general saying that "time and tide wait for no man." This common English proverb literally means that no one can stop the passing of time, hence we should not delay.

If this expression is true, then it will be right to say that "wise use of the 24 hours available in a day is the most important investment in life."

In this short chapter, I discuss the importance of time, time and money investment towards exam preparation. I repeated the word *time* to emphasize that time is more important than money.

It all starts with commitment

If you are truly serious about getting a professional certification, then you must invest your time and money in the course materials, research, networking, etc.

Of course, the common excuse is "I don't have money to buy all these materials." However, I want to remind you again, the most valuable investment in education is time and not money.

This comment does not mean that money is not needed, but you will agree with me now or later that it is the failure to invest time that causes most people to fail their exams.

Talk to your spouse and work supervisor

I also recommend that you speak to your line manager and spouse as part of managing your time commitment and money. Explain the importance of the qualification to them.

Your supervisor can support you in managing your studies. This may include assigning you to tasks that are related to the course and be considerate with your work schedule. Many companies also provide one-week paid exam leave and even pay the tuition or exam fees for professional courses.

Your spouse or better-half is a partner. Therefore, they should be aware of other important time or money commitment to gain their support and understanding.

Invest some money

For anyone to sit professional exams, they must pay the examination fees, and, in some cases, the tuition fees as well. Those with the financial ability also consider investing in different related books, magazines, online libraries, seminars, review courses, etc. This supports their understanding of the subject or the profession.

However, if you want to invest in any course, be prepared to invest in the right materials. I saw many students reading for an exam in 2009 while using books published in 2006. For reality's sake, these professional bodies always want to be current and up to date, and so do their exams.

It is strongly recommended that you buy the current study text and question banks from an approved provider to ensure your exam success. These providers have the most up-to-date content and syllabus coverage. Their tests, quizzes, and other support materials are designed to help you prepare for the relevant module. They update their books with the current syllabus, question styles, and exam formats. Their practice questions and answers are also updated to ensure that you are fully prepared for the paper.

Therefore, using an old textbook could risk you reading an outdated concept or exam format. For instance, tax rates and law keeps on changing on an annual basis. The officially updated textbooks cover such changes.

Furthermore, spending time and money on additional seminars or training could also support your success in a professional exam. You may have read in the introduction that I didn't attend any classroom lectures for any of the ACCA professional exams, and yet I passed these papers at the first sitting. Well, there was something I did for one of the advanced course papers - distance learning course.

When I was studying for the Advanced Taxation (UK), I had to borrow some money from a bank. I used this to enrol in a distance learning course with Kaplan Financial Training (UK), one of the Approved Learning Providers and publisher of ACCA course materials. I also attended a taxation seminar organised by the Gambia Revenue Authority and ACCA. These two events expanded my horizon of the tax system in both the UK and the Gambia. I am certain that without the seminar and distance learning support, I would have struggled with that tax paper.

Time investment has no substitute

Whether you have enough funds or not, money is never a substitute for the time investment required to succeed in any exam.

There are many low-income earners (including me) who passed exams with flying colours, and there are rich ones who failed due to the poor investment of time - the working capital.

Without time investment, a good lecturer, a school, or money cannot guarantee anyone's exam success. You must seriously plan to use your time and invest at least a few hours of a day in reading, practising, and research.

According to one study conducted by Common Sense Media in 2015, an average teenager in the United States of America spends about nine hours on social media every day. This estimate excludes the number of times spent watching TV or being active on other social networks. Furthermore, many teens use the social media while studying, and most think it has no effect on the quality of their study.

Additionally, some die-hard sports fans can remember all the upcoming matches of their favourite teams or the history of their best players, yet they find it difficult to remember their study notes. Why? Because they have committed their mind, time, and even money to know about these players and the events surrounding their life.

Frankly, it is unfair to spend the whole day on other activities, such as watching TV or surfing the social media and only spend a few last minutes of the night to study notes.

Excellent students sacrifice more of their time to research, study, and revise their course notes, while average students use more of their time to play, browse unrelated websites, etc.

> *If you only use your free time to read and practise notes, then expect only poor marks from the examiners.*

Good students are always disciplined about how they use their time before and during the examination.

Why would someone wait until the last few days before starting to study for the exams? Lack of commitment - simple. This last-minute hustle can be fruitless in most cases as the mind would be under pressure to read, understand, and at the same time think about the repercussions of exam failure.

You should plan your days with activities to include time to read, relax, network, etc. A study timetable will help you achieve this goal. See Chapter 6 for details.

M.A.N.S.A. is a lifestyle and not a king

Many people call me *MANSA* which literally means "King" in Mandinka, one of the many languages of Africa.

MANSA is an acronym I developed in my high school days. It means **M**anagement as an **A**ttitude of a **N**imble **S**tudent in his **A**ctivities.

As a student from a low-income background, my parents could not afford to pay for private lessons, nor access to the internet. Yet I graduated with Grade A (distinction) in five subjects out of the eight I sat during my final year in high school, i.e. the West African Senior School Certificate Examination in 2003.

In fact, in most cases, I used to borrow books from my classmates. Self-discipline, focus, and active time management through timetables were the secrets of my exam success in school.

The same habits continued even after high school. While reading for the CAT and ACCA exams, I was working in a commercial bank (in the busy finance or operations department for that matter). If you have ever worked for a commercial bank in Africa, you will understand that the finance and operations department usually works very late. With these work-related challenges, time, and tiredness, I always ensured that my study timetables were not severely affected.

If I could pass all my ACCA papers with a full-time banking job and without attending classes, so can you. You may have some late-night reading or early morning devotions. You may miss some of your favourite TV shows, but think about the possibilities that will emerge from being professionally certified. They will outweigh the small time and money investments that you may temporarily give up.

So, do it for yourself and invest some money and more time, and you will pass that important exam.

Summary and action plans

In this chapter, you have learnt the key investment required to pass any exam. A little money and more time investment. Perform the following assessments as you prepare for your next paper or course.

- List the essential materials and sources of information that will help your studies

- Assess how much money investment is needed to access these materials and information

- Review the number of other social and personal events you have to sacrifice for the study

CHAPTER 3

CHOOSE A SUITABLE LEARNING METHOD

"It is common sense to take a method and try it. If it fails, admit it frankly and try another. But above all, try something." **—Franklin D. Roosevelt, 32nd President of the United States of America**

After you have made up your mind to become a professional through certification, the next critical step is to choose the key learning style that will work for you. Everyone has a different learning style, and understanding yours will be a great self-awareness exercise.

Some people enjoy classroom lectures, while others would rather read a textbook or listen to audios. However, most people combine one or two learning methods, depending on the subject and their situation.

Standard learning methods

Although the advance in technology continues to make the old learning styles less relevant, the most common learning methods can fall into four main categories for professional courses:

- Live classroom lectures

- Self-studies

- Distance and e-learning

- Practice

This chapter focuses on the first three methods. You will learn more about the practical approach in Chapter 7, which is learning by doing.

Classroom lectures

This is the oldest and most common method of learning. It requires a high amount of investment of time and money.

Most professional qualifications focus their syllabus and exam goals on the practical applications of knowledge. Classroom lectures provide this benefit as presenters share their personal experiences on the subject.

Lecturers can help students understand a particular area of the topic; they give you the opportunity to discuss and interact. You can ask questions and interact with other students through question-and-answer sessions.

Classroom or live lectures were once the most common learning methods, but nowadays distance learning and online courses seem to be taking the lead.

Self-study

Many busy professionals use the self-study approach with approved textbooks, journals, and the internet to acquire new qualifications.

With self-study, you become your own lecturer, but sometimes you may consult others. You do not have to attend classes.

Nonetheless, self-study also requires some experience, a good foundation knowledge of the subject, and self-discipline. These prerequisites will increase your chances of success in examinations.

I used self-study with the support of the internet for most of my professional courses. I could not afford to leave my job in the pursuit of my professional qualifications.

Distance and e-learning

Distance learning is a version of self-study where you buy course materials, and have the support of tutors via telephone or online platforms. You have access to the provider's forums where you can discuss issues or ideas with other students and your lecturers.

While most distance learning has the downside of not getting instant answers from tutors, it is suitable for those who cannot attend classroom lectures due to lack of funding or nature of their work. Online learning can also give you access to virtual classmates from diverse backgrounds through discussion forums.

Unlike classroom lectures, remember that if you do not ask for help when you need it, your distance learning tutor may never know that you need support.

There are other forms of distance learning, such as live or recorded webinars and podcasts.

Which learning method works?

Which method to choose depends on the individual situation, such as self-awareness, availability of funding, and nature of work.

Awareness of how you successfully retain facts and principles can help you effectively study your coursework. For example, some people learn better when walking around while they study; others listen to music or make use of visual aids.

Sometimes it is best to combine a number of learning methods. When I was studying for the accounting technician course, I used live lectures for the foundation, but most of my higher levels were self-study. Again, all my MBA papers and the advanced taxation paper in ACCA course were 100% distance learning.

If you are a busy person and cannot commit to research, then I would recommend live lectures or distance learning. The tutors can provide a guide, summary notes, but you still have to study.

Furthermore, you may adopt different learning methods for different papers or levels of the same qualification. It does not have to be only one method. You may decide to study the Foundation course through self-study, the Intermediate programme via distance learning, and the Advanced course through classroom lectures.

Summary and action plans

There are many learning methods available to study professional courses. However, it is important that you give some serious thought to which method would be most suitable for you. Think about what works for you, how effective you are at time management and self-study, and what your economic conditions are.

Ask yourself the following questions as you decide on the learning method:

- Do you have the time to attend classroom lectures?

- Is there any suitable nearby institution that offers lectures?

- What is the estimated cost of each learning method, and which one can you afford?

- Do you have the available tools to attend online or distance learning courses?

- Which method is suitable for you?

PART 2

GET SET

"If you are not willing to learn, no one can help you. If you are determined to learn, no one can stop you." —Zig Ziglar, American author, salesman, and motivational speaker.

CHAPTER 4

UNDERSTAND THE EXAM STRUCTURE AND MARKING SCHEME

Course syllabuses are like road maps which give students direction towards the examination.

The best way to start learning any course is to review the curriculum and appreciate the various sections. In this chapter, you will learn:

- The importance of the exam syllabus and guidance

- Important elements to consider in syllabus review

- Other sources of information about the examination

The syllabus and guidelines

Every professional paper has objectives which form the content of the syllabus and exam questions. In some cases, the curriculum also includes detailed instructions and sample exam questions with model answers.

However, many students continue to fail exams because they lack a proper understanding of the study guide or the examination structure.

For some professional bodies, the study guidelines provide marks allocation per topic or section of the syllabus. For instance, the Chartered Financial

Analyst Program (CFA) provides a list of subject areas and estimated exam weight for all the three levels. This weighting indicates the importance of the section in the syllabus.

Again, if there is any question allocation for a particular section of the curriculum, is the examiner following it? The best thing to do is to review the most recent past exam questions and answers. This will provide you with a clear picture of how the course will be assessed as well as the likely question styles that you could see in the real exam.

In professional qualifications, examiners are not only interested in the definition of the terms and concepts but also in how these concepts are applied in real situations. You should expect a question on multiple choice, scenarios, case studies, essay, all geared towards knowledge application.

Some study guidelines also indicate the required knowledge level on complex topics. For instance, students reading taxation at the foundation level can be expected to calculate basic personal income tax. However, this level may not be required to calculate advanced personal tax issues such as inheritance tax and retirement tax planning. You can learn the required knowledge level for each paper through a syllabus review.

Many professional bodies also provide an examiner's report following the publication of the exam results for each session. This report does not only discuss the students' performances but also highlights the common subject areas in which candidates performed poorly. For instance, the ACCA examiners' report usually presents the key points markers are looking for while marking the exam scripts. I always read such reports for each paper, and sometimes I found some interesting exam tips.

What about the course textbooks?

Some professional bodies, such as the CPA, provide the course syllabus and guidelines for each paper. However, they do not prepare or author the official textbooks. Some associations recommend two or three publishers, but they do not guarantee that those publishers' content covers 100% of the syllabus, or their text explanation is best for every student.

Even with the courses that provide their original textbooks upon registration, they cannot guarantee that such books are best for your learning requirement.

For the reasons mentioned above, it is sometimes better to combine course notes or textbooks from different publishers. Compare them and prepare your study notes.

A syllabus or study guide is like a contract between the student and the examination body. It should be the reference point for any student or lecturer. When preparing exam questions, examiners are expected to look at the syllabus, not the textbooks.

You should spend a day or so to compare the content of your textbooks with the examination guide. This helps you trace the relevant topics in the book.

Some professional bodies examine current or emerging affairs, such as new standards issued by international organisations. For instance, an accounting profession may examine an exposure draft issued by the International Accounting Standard Board (IASB). Similarly, project management could consider new standards published by the International Organization for Standardization (ISO), and the same applies to the Bar examination.

Syllabus review will help you understand to what extent current affairs are examinable in the paper.

Official magazine and newsletters

One of the standard benefits of being a student or member of professional bodies is the constant supply of relevant and updated information through journals and newsletters.

While these platforms provide news affecting the profession, there are usually many technical articles and interviews that could help students understand a particular aspect of the examinable topics. New articles and opinions could be very relevant in areas that continually face new updates, such as accounting standards, tax laws, corporate governance, and scientific research.

Again, I have read many articles in both the student and member's magazine published by the ACCA. Some of the writers use real case studies and stories, which make learning easier.

The examiners and experienced professionals write some of these technical articles. In some instances, they explain an important topic or syllabus changes in a better way than the recommended textbooks.

Be familiar with the exam format

It is imperative to understand the exam format of every paper or module. Will the exam be set as an essay, case studies, or multiple-choice questions? Are all the questions compulsory, or will students have to choose among several questions?

If the examiner asks you to answer four out of six questions, then attempting only three could make you fail the paper.

Some professional courses, such as ISO 27001, are based on an 'open book' exam. That means the official course textbooks are allowed into the exam hall. This may sound easier as you have the right to look for the answer in the textbook. However, open book exams are known to put students under lots of pressure as they are often quite difficult. It requires critical time management during the exam.

"An open book exam requires a genuine understanding of the material and be able to interpret, think critically, and present an organised and well-written answer." **— Dr V.K.Maheshwari, Former Principal, K.L.D.A.V.(P.G.) College, Roorkee, India.**

Above all, with a good understanding of the syllabus and course materials, you can succeed in any exam.

Summary and action plans

In conclusion, you can increase your chances of exam success by understanding the course syllabus and structure of the exam questions.

You can understand the exam structure through the following:

- Review the syllabuses and study guides for each course before your first class or reading

- Mark out the exam structure, particularly the allocation of questions to sections, if applicable

- Review two to three past papers to link the exam guide to the actual exam

- If the examiners' reports are available, then read some of the feedback to learn the mistakes made by students or examiners' expectations.

- Technical articles from the official magazine and blogs can also support your understanding of the examinable areas

- Check online student forums and communities that help learners.

CHAPTER 5

PREPARE PERSONAL STUDY NOTES

Putting together your own study materials is one of the effective ways of learning. It is the act of summarising the key points of a lecture or textbook. As you will learn later in this chapter, personal study notes help to remember course materials.

Personal study materials have been useful to students during reading and the revision period.

For instance, during last-minute revision, it is not always feasible to read the whole textbook.

Study notes help you focus on the most relevant information to support your understanding of the topic. As you rearrange and write the information, the process helps your working memory to quickly recall these key points when needed.

This chapter discusses the common methods students can use to prepare own study notes from a lecture or textbook. It also examines some of the principles of effective note-taking.

How to read textbooks and take notes

There are many methods for reading techniques. However, the most common system is the SQ3R (Survey, Question, Read, Recall and Review). It is a popular active reading method that helps boost students' understanding. It was developed by Francis Pleasant Robinson (1906-1983) in his book *Effective Study*. Robinson was a professor of psychology at Ohio State University in the USA.

Nonetheless, I prefer to read and take notes using another method that is similar to the SQ3R, as discussed in the steps below:

Scan - First introduce yourself to the material through a quick scan. Glance through the headings, introduction, diagrams, and pictures. You can also read the final paragraph or summary points, if there are any. This will give you the main idea about the topic you are about to read.

Read - The next step is to read the material by sections or subheadings. I prefer to read twice before moving on to the third step. The first reading will be active, while the second will involve highlighting the vital information in the section. At this stage, you need to relax and focus.

Take summary notes - With the highlighted information, you can make personal summary notes in your own words. Again, concentrate on the most relevant information.

You can take notes using simple summary points or mind maps. We will discuss each method in more detail later in this chapter.

Review - After reading a few sections or even a short chapter, you should review your summary notes. At this stage, you should test your memory by reciting the major points of the section or chapter.

It will be helpful if you could create some potential test questions on the topic and try to answer them during the review stage. You can try to replicate the diagrams, writing the formulas, or recite the steps. You should also relate the material to a case study or scenario.

Implementing these steps as you read and summarize the notes, will help you prepare good study materials and easy recall of the key concepts in revision and exams.

The principles of effective note-taking

The principle of developing good study notes depends on the learning method and individual situation. However, some general principles can be applied to most cases. I have summarised these general note tips below:

1. Don't be late for lectures - The lecture objective and introduction happen at the beginning. Lecturers' introduction can affect how you take notes.

2. Sit in the front or second row - You can hear the lecturer's voice more clearly, and maybe this is one reason why most high-performing students don't usually sit at the back of the classroom.

3. Use headings and subheadings - This helps you understand the relationship between two or more ideas. For example, the Human Body System could be the main heading, while the Respiratory System could be a subheading. The main heading could use numbers and subheadings use alphabets.

4. Be an active listener or reader - In a lecture or reading room, you must be active to write good study notes, and you have to be focused to be an active listener.

5. Notes should be brief and eligible for you to read.

6. Use your own words to summarise - The use of your own words is what helps you remember faster.

7. Underline or mark the keywords - Highlight the important words and phrases as you read or write the notes.

8. Illustrations, examples, and diagrams can be helpful.

9. Lecture cues - Pay attention to the lecturer's cues through their emphasis on repetition, tone, and time spent on discussion or diagrams.

10. *Use abbreviations and shorthand to save time,* i.e. instead of writing human resources management, just use HRM.

11. Read the notes straight after the class, and complete them with any missing information.

12. Follow-up research - Do a follow-up research on anything that you think is really important. Google and the library are your friends. Do more research on areas that are not clear from the lecture or textbook.

Study note-taking methods

Now that we have discussed the principles of taking notes, let's discuss some of the common methods. There are many ways of preparing study notes; however, below are the two approaches I found useful throughout my professional studies: Summary notes and mind maps.

Summary notes

Preparing summary notes is one of the most common study skills used by most successful students. Yet, lots of average students rely on reading the whole textbook or lecture handout.

Note-taking involves preparing a summarised version of a textbook, handout, or classroom lecture in your own words so you can easily remember them. It primarily helps learners document the course content to better understand it at a later review.

As explained earlier, the key benefit of note-taking is to select the most important concepts and link them to other pieces of information. It can be beneficial to the extent that you rewrite, organise, and make sense of the idea while taking notes.

You should also link up points, headings through arrows, or number references.

For example, if Section 2.1 and Section 4.3 are closely related, I make references by writing something like "see 4.3" at the end of the Section 2.1 heading. In this way, I know reading one section can help me understand the other.

However, many students adopt a less efficient method by rewriting almost everything. You should only focus on the important concepts and keywords that you need to remember during revision and examinations. I found phrases more useful than sentences.

Mind maps

Mind maps (sometimes called *thought maps*) are a creative and visual way of organizing information around a central subject. They can help you link ideas and see a clear relationship between a heading, subheading, and the whole topic.

This description reminds me of the late Steve Jobs, former CEO of Apple who said:

> *"Creativity is just connecting things. When you ask creative people how they did something, they feel a little guilty because they didn't really do it, they just saw something."*

Mind maps can help you to be more creative, and easily remember course notes compared to traditional summary notes. Studying with mind maps can also help the brain absorb complex information by focusing on the necessary information.

You can review your mind maps before the exam and try to test if you can recall the key terms, factors, reasoning, and flow of the subject. This makes them an efficient revision tool.

In the examination hall, one can sketch a mind map on the question paper before beginning the task. This will help you create a good action plan of what needs to be done.

A mind map can be drawn with a pen and paper or by using a computer. I prefer to start with pen and paper, even if I later transfer it to a laptop. Why? There is a scientific study that says that it is easier to recall what you have handwritten than what you type with a keyboard.

If you have never seen a mind map before, which I doubt, simply visit Google and go to the image tab of the search result.

Mind maps can be drawn using a few easy steps as discussed below. In this example, we aim to draw a mind map for the "elements of company financial statements."

1. Pick up a blank page.

2. Write the title of the topic in the centre of the paper. For this purpose " elements of financial statements."

3. Move away from the centre and add the subheadings or keywords to the subject. Again, using our example, we will add income statement, balance sheet, cash flow statement, etc.

4. Insert the key information for each subheading, e.g. under the balance sheet, we can add assets, liabilities, capital, etc.

5. Add a further explanation to the subheading, e.g. under assets, we can point to current assets, non-current assets, etc.

6. We can add more information if necessary. We can add stock and cash to the current assets in our example.

You can use colours on related keywords, which also makes the map visually stimulating. The use of your own words, symbols, and images in place of the subject keywords can also help you reinforce points and aid recall.

Find the incomplete image of our mind map in the figure below:

Other methods

Mind maps and summary notes are the most common methods to prepare personal study notes. However, there are other methods, the use of which depends on the subject.

- Tables

- Flowcharts

- Graphs

- Diagrams etc.

A flowchart would be the best to summarise a process or steps if such a layout can be tested in an exam question. Similarly, some calculation subjects may be best summarised in the form of a table. I found diagrams useful for science subjects.

Which method works better?

I prefer to use the combination of both mind maps and summary notes. In most cases, I usually start with summary notes and then convert them to mind maps. This enables me to rewrite the same concept twice in my own words. At the time of studying, I didn't even know there were advantages to handwritten notes.

Nonetheless, according to Michael C. Friedman of Harvard University in the USA, good note taking practices can lead to efficient study practices, better course outcomes, and improved retention of content beyond a course's conclusion.

Notes can be taken using a pen and paper approach or applications like Evernote, Google Doc or Microsoft Word.

A new study by Pam Mueller and Daniel Oppenheimer of Princeton University and The University of California, Los Angeles, respectively demonstrates that students who write out their notes by hand, actually learn more than those who type their notes on laptops. Across three experiments, Mueller and Oppenheimer had students take notes and tested their memory for a general understanding of the notes on different subjects, and their ability to recall the information.

However, in each study, those who wrote out notes by hand had a good conceptual understanding and integrating the material than those who used laptops.

This means that it is easier for the brain to recall handwritten notes than the ones printed as a handout or even typed. It signals that taking notes by hand forces the brain to engage in some mental activity which helps understanding and retention.

It is possible that my handwritten notes and mind maps were some of the methods that helped me quickly recall concepts and ideas during my exams.

Whichever method you decide to use, I want you to understand that study notes preparation can assist you in two ways. First, it is easy for the brain to recall your written notes. Second, you can revise your summary notes instead of having to open the whole textbook when the exam day is near.

It is important to appreciate that one technique may be more suitable to your natural learning style than another one. Furthermore, some methods may be more appropriate for certain subjects. For example, mind maps can be useful to display complex information, but tables and diagrams are better for some papers.

Remember, everyone has different suitable learning methods - what works for a friend may not work for you. Use the method that works for you as long as it's effective and delivers results.

Summary and action plans

Whether it is a mind map or bullet point notes, personal study notes can aid revision. If you want to improve your understanding of a textbook, then prepare personal study notes.

- Review your coursebook and decide on your note taking strategy

- Prepare the notes using one or more methods

- Highlight the key ideas or formulas in your notes

This takes us to the next chapter, which talks about how to remember key ideas and formulas. A good study note can help you remember ideas. However, there are other proven techniques for remembering new concepts and formulas.

CHAPTER 6

REMEMBER THE KEY IDEAS AND FORMULAS

Many professional exam papers require the use of formulas or standard procedures in responding to exam questions. The complex formulas are sometimes given by the examiner, and you are only expected to apply them to the case study. This is very common in calculation courses.

However, if you read past exam questions, you will find that some formulas are not given as part of the exam questions. For such papers, you should learn how to construct and apply formulas in the exam.

It is important that you recall the construction and application of formulas, as your success in some exams will largely depend on them. With a better understanding of the formulas used, the interpretation of the final result and conclusion should be a straightforward exercise.

How can you remember formulas, steps, and procedures? The answer is the focus of this chapter.

Break it into components

One of the simple methods to remember a formula is to break it into parts. Then study and practise each element separately, and try to build back to the original formula.

It is advisable to calculate solutions through the elements of the formula instead of a single, complicated step. This will help you learn the formula through a process that involves multiple steps instead of one complex and ugly formula. Of course, most formulas look ugly to people who think they are difficult.

For instance, one common formula in statistics and finance is the Pearson correlation coefficient. I always found it easier to break this formula into four different components and calculate their values. The results are then put into the master formula.

If your exam is based on calculations, try this method with the complicated formulas. You will learn that every complex formula is made up of several simple components.

Flash cards

A flash card can be described as a handy card that contains information using numbers, words, or pictures to aid learning. In the primary school, we used to have a question on one side of the flash card and the answer on the other. They are also useful for university students.

Flash cards can be used to introduce new vocabulary for a clear understanding of the word or concept. They help studies through what experts call *active recall*, one of the practices through which the brain learns most effectively. With active recall, you stimulate the brain to remember the information.

For example, reading a book and answering the question, 'Where is the capital of the Gambia?' is active recall compared to just reading a book about the Gambia and Banjul with no action.

You can easily memorise formulas written on the flash cards by hanging them somewhere you often see. This could be your study, bedroom or the background image of your laptop. You should go through the card frequently as this will influence your ability to quickly remember the information.

Flash cards are good for active recall, but they also have some challenges. Time is required to create cards for many concepts and formulas for each paper, although there are many flash card tools and sites online to help with this.

Use mnemonics, acronyms, and abbreviations

Mnemonics are techniques used to encode information in a way that makes it easy to recall. It's another way of memorizing information so that the brain can easily remember it in the future.

Do you remember the primary school rhyme '30 days hath September, April, June, and November?' This rhyme is used for remembering the number of days in each calendar month.

Another mnemonic that is used for approximating the digits of Pi is "How I wish I could recollect Pi." Counting the number of letters in each word gives the sequence 3,1,4,1,5,9,2,6, which is the number of Pi.

Mnemonics help you to quickly recall ideas, formulas, or lists through the use of phrases and short songs. If there are no standard mnemonics for the subject you are studying, then think and develop ones for yourself. Maybe, one day, yours could be the standard used by other students.

Your mnemonic should be something memorable. Therefore, you should imagine a code that can be associated with something positive, pleasant, or even funny. The idea is to use a vivid mental image, which the brain can recall when you need the information.

When testing an internal control system in a professional audit examination, there are certain tests an auditor should consider. When I was studying, we used to recall the keywords of these procedures through the mnemonic SPAM SOAP, whose full meaning is:

S – Segregation of duties

P – Physical controls

A – Authorization and approval

M – Management controls

S – Supervisory controls

O – Organization as a control

A – Arithmetical and accounting controls

P – Personnel controls

If an exam question asked about internal control tests or procedures, you could start by listing the above mnemonic. Then write a detailed explanation of each element and back them up with some examples.

Another way of remembering formulas and ideas is to use acronyms. With this method, you can either use the general and common abbreviations such as SWOT, CAPM, PESTLE, or create your own.

However, it is important to note that while mnemonics and acronyms may not help you to understand the study material, they do help you to easily recall the details you need in exams, for instance, the names of the 8 planets in the solar system and lists of laws. For this reason, mnemonics are invaluable in helping you 'cram' for an exam.

Audio records

Another way to help you remember the key ideas is by listening to the audio recording of a lecture or summary note. Some courses provide summary audios. If there are none available, then use your smartphone or a similar device to record the key points yourself. You can listen to these audios several times during your free time, such as on a flight and on a bus.

Summary and action plans

Remembering important formulas and concepts can help you write good points in the exam. Try the following tasks at the beginning of your studies:

- Identify the essential formulas and steps you need to understand for the paper.

- Choose the most suitable approach that will aid you to understand the formulas and steps, for example, flash card, audio, and mnemonics.

- Prepare the materials using the method identified above.

- Do this for every subject or paper.

The study notes preparation and recalls are crucial to understanding the course material. Nonetheless, you can also learn the course information through practical application. You will learn and apply the knowledge.

CHAPTER 7

LEARN THE PRACTICAL APPLICATION OF THE NOTES

'By three methods we may learn wisdom: First, by reflection, which is noblest; Second, by imitation, which is easiest; and third by experience, which is the bitterest.' —**Confucius, Chinese philosopher and teacher**

One of the primary reasons why professional qualifications are assumed to be difficult is that most people cannot easily relate the textbooks, lecture notes, and examination questions to real-world issues. Nonetheless, professional bodies set certifications to help members tackle real problems.

You can read and revise the same material several times. However, understanding it can be difficult if your mind cannot relate the content to practical life issues. This can be difficult for most students who have little or no working experience. Yet the exam questions are the same for both experienced and inexperienced students.

It is the basis of this reason that most MBA schools and professional courses recommend that students acquire a few months' or years' working experience before enrolling in their programmes.

If you want to understand professional textbooks, you must look for practical ways to apply or relate the knowledge. Unlike most academic courses, professional courses expect you to test and apply the learned concepts to office, community, personal, and case study problems.

In fact, most professional bodies would never award you full membership, even after passing the exams, without the relevant working experience. This membership requirement confirms the importance of working experience to professional bodies.

There are three main opportunities to practise or relate your course notes to real-life issues:

Ask the experts

For every professional exam you plan to sit, it is most likely that someone has done that exam before or is doing work activities that are similar to the content of the syllabus. These experts can help you understand some topics of the subject. All you have to do is network and ask the right questions, and you will learn something from them.

If you are like most people, you might be afraid to ask due to the fear of rejection or looking foolish in front of the individual. In reality, the truth is that most successful people are willing to share their experience and knowledge if you ask in the right way.

Nonetheless, let me share with you a good way to handle rejection before it even appears. I want you to always see rejection as a myth. Let me put it this way: If you asked John to explain a topic to you and he said no, you haven't lost anything. You are the same person as before you asked. If one person rejects you, then look for another person.

However, it is advisable to read and research the topic before you visit these busy professionals for any help. Understand the basic concept of the subject, as they will have other things to do. Even if the person is your lecturer, they might interpret it as lack of commitment on your side.

Imagine, for a minute, that you are a practising certified human resources professional, and two human resources students approached you for help. One person said he didn't understand anything about the human resources compensation calculation and the other person said she didn't get the relationship between gross pay and net pay. Which of these two students is easier to help? Of course, it is the second person who is more precise and clear.

Clarity and brevity will directly affect other peoples willingness to help on any subject.

The more you ask for help on a specific issue, the easier it is to help you.

I used to find it difficult to understand the formula of Weighted Average Cost of Capital (WACC) until I met the late Cherno Jallow (rest in peace). Cherno was a chartered accountant and managing partner of DT Associates, a correspondent firm of Deloitte and Touche in the Gambia. His firm performed a valuation consultancy for my employer in 2008. During our initial interaction, I informed Cherno that I was pursuing a professional accounting qualification. He was glad and opened his doors for any support.

As part of the final report, his team included WACC computation. I used the opportunity and asked him how they derived the cost of equity and cost of debt for valuation purposes. These are the two key components of cost of capital. He explained the concept, formula, and practical application of WACC. This was how the WACC permanently stuck in my mind.

I also talked to lawyers and technology experts when reading business law and information management systems respectively as part of my accounting qualifications.

So, if you are reading for the CFA qualification and cannot understand what influences the use of a particular method for investment valuation, you can ask an experienced analyst or a CFA charter holder. These experts can explain how they choose an appropriate method in their appraisal process.

Similarly, a human resource manager will be able to explain the factors that influence them to use more external recruitment than internal recruitment when filling a vacant position at the senior level.

Do it yourself

The secret to being an excellent student is not just going to classes or reading the textbooks; it's also learning by practising. "Doing" is one of the best ways to learn anything. This has been my strategy, not just with passing exams, but learning new software and doing office work.

> *'I hear and I forget. I see and I remember. I do and I understand.'*
> **—Confucius**

When I was reading for the corporate reporting paper of ACCA level 3, I learned the application of some complex accounting standards through the real financial statements we prepared in the office.

I first studied the published financial statement of Ecobank Group, which was prepared using the international financial reporting standard (IFRS). The activities involved reading all the notes to the accounts, including accounting policies, disclosures, and management reports. Then I ensured my full participation in the preparation of the annual reports (IFRS) for that year.

This approach helped my understanding of financial reporting under IFRS, which was the key component of the ACCA paper I was studying for.

I used a similar approach to understand other topics, such as overhead cost sharing, financial statement analysis, project management, and information security.

Sometimes the course content may not directly relate to your office work. However, you can offer to work in other departments through short assignments or internships.

Above all, whatever course or certification you are pursuing, learning by doing can help you understand and apply the course content.

Learn beyond the textbooks

Professional students are always expected to read more widely than the textbooks and tutors' manuals. Supplementary reading helps students consolidate their knowledge in any subject. You are therefore advised to read related journals, watch TV shows, and join online forums and magazines.

A regular reading of high-quality industry journals can help you link the study materials to practical ideas. This can enhance your understanding and, therefore, your chances of success in the examination.

An industry journal may have explained issues using stories and case studies. You may have heard that when storytelling is formalised in meaningful ways, it can turn into an opportunity to learn as it encourages both reflection and a deeper understanding of the topic; it also stimulates critical thinking skills.

The journals and magazines may also help you understand current issues which relate to the profession. For instance, the idea of Britain exiting the European Union (BREXIT) will affect many professions, including legal, labour market, and trade. So, do not be surprised if a professional examination asks you to discuss the effect of Brexit on your client business or industry.

Credit risk management was one of the complex modules in my MBA course. I had never worked in credit management, and the syllabus required us to understand credit assessment models used by credit rating agencies. I had to read professional risk management magazines and research papers to understand some of the models. With this process, I was able to understand concepts that the official course text did not explain very well.

All the top professional bodies provide periodic magazines or E-zines for their students and members. Students can benefit from the publications by reading the related case studies, articles, and interviews.

Summary and action plans

Learning by doing has helped many students understand their course notes. You have the option to seek expert help, do it yourself or read related magazines. Perform the exercises below for each paper at the beginning of the course:

- List the key syllabus areas that may require the aid of practical knowledge

- List the names of professionals, experts, and magazines that may help you understand the areas

- Link each critical area to either an experienced expert, online forum, or magazine

- Start to engage the experts and agree on the modalities

You can prepare the best study notes or get help from experts, but your success in any exam will be limited if you do not review your notes.

CHAPTER 8

STUDY AND REVISE YOUR NOTES

'Success is a matter of understanding and religiously practising specific, simple habits that always lead to success.'—**Robert J Ringer Author of Million Dollar Habits.**

As the saying goes, 'Fail to prepare, then prepare to fail.' It is better to be prepared through studies than the last-minute cramming during a few nights before the exam. Frequent studies can help you get prepared on time and discover any topic of the course that may need more practice.

Did you know that the word *student* came from the word *study*? In other words, you cannot be a student without studying. The habit of consistent studying is what differentiates a successful student from the rest. No one can achieve success in school if they are unwilling to make personal sacrifices.

Without a doubt, the key to success in life is to get your priorities right. As a student, your priorities should be to study and learn. You may be intelligent and wealthy but only repeated studies can make you successful in your examinations.

'Some people say I am smart, some say I am intelligent. However, my most powerful secret is the willingness to study and practise whatever I want to learn.'

I was not the most intelligent person in my high school class, but my hard work helped me come first in the class throughout my 3 years at Nusrat High School.

> *'Hard work can beat intelligent if intelligent fails to work hard.'*
> **—Unknown**

This quote confirms that in any class or life endeavour, intelligent or talent counts, but hard work puts you right up there. It is similar to the case of a good idea and action. The success of any good ideas depends on the execution.

To efficiently study for success even beyond the examination hall, let's discuss some guidelines for every professional student:

Prepare a workable study plan

One of the effective ways of succeeding in education is to develop a learning plan. This starts with reading, revision, and a practising schedule. Timetables can help you achieve your goals and priorities in the limited available time.

Where do you start?

You need to first identify the key date, which is the examination date. Then set a deadline by which you must finish reading the course material and complete the mock test. Prepare a study timetable using these two important dates.

For instance, I always set four weeks prior to the exam as my target date to complete the syllabus and revision. During these four weeks, I usually attempted one or two mock exams and revised the most difficult parts of the course.

It is important you ensure the timetables are balanced with your other daily activities, particularly if you are working and at the same time studying a course. Your study schedule should be realistic and set for each subject and with the objective of which topics to cover.

I used to set and review timetables monthly, as this gave me the opportunity to adjust between subjects and provide more time for the topics that were not on schedule or not well understood. I am good at numbers, so most of my timetables favour reading topics. You always have limited time, so focus on those areas of the subjects that need the most attention, not the most exciting or the topic you like best.

Remember it is important to study frequently, as it takes repeated studies to move information into the long-term memory, according to scientific findings.

In an interview with Carmine Gallo, Dr Pascale Michelon, an adjunct professor at Washington University in St. Louis, said, " We all get better at what we do if we do it repeatedly."

Learning and repeating build new pathways in the brain that become more activated and efficient the more they are used.

Olayinka Oseni, Nigeria ACCA Joint Winner for P1 June 2013, also has this to say:

> *"Attempt as many questions as possible and try to cover the entire syllabus. I solved all the questions in my exam kit at least three times to make sure I had*

a sound grasp of the different concepts and principles. I also tried as much as possible to cover most of the topics in the Study Guide. Additionally, I set up a study plan at the beginning of my studies to help me stay focused and keep on track."

Understand the best time to study

The best study time for each individual depends on a number of lifestyle factors. This could be your natural sleeping patterns, family responsibilities, working status, etc. An adult with busy working schedules during the day will find that either early morning or night times are far better suited than the late afternoon.

Additionally, some people are night owls, and others can only effectively study during the day. It is important to note that daytime studies allow you to visit libraries or discuss with friends without interrupting your natural sleep cycle. However, the night also gives you a peaceful and quiet environment.

While many students study during the night due to family and work commitment, I always prefer the early morning. I read before leaving for work, or I get to work early in the morning and read before official operations start. I do also read during the night, but morning time seems to be more effective for me. Maybe it is the result of the general fact that when you are rested and wake up fresh in the morning, your brain functions better, and you can easily absorb more information and solve problems.

So, whether you're a night owl or daytime star, you should study in your own time and at your own pace.

Study environment matters – context-dependent memory

A suitable place to study is best in an atmosphere that is similar to the exam hall. It should be quiet and free from interruptions.

Do you know the scientific phenomenon called *"context-dependent memory?"* According to this theory, people tend to recall information better when the context that is present during learning and retrieval are similar.

The results of studies investigating context-dependent memory have frequently shown that memory for information learned in one environment (e.g. classroom) is improved when remembering takes place in the same or very similar sitting. – Jennifer Mishra, University of Northern Iowa.

The context-dependent memory theory is practised in many other professions other than schools. For example, professional football clubs may organize test matches with other clubs before their live soccer competition. Similarly, some musicians perform a test show at the same venue as their live show. This approach builds the self-confidence of the artist and players as the practice environment and real environment are the same.

On the basis of the context-dependent memory findings, it is best to study in an environment that is very similar to the exam hall. A quiet room or library would be a most suitable study place for a professional exam.

Start it with motivation

Feeling motivated and interested in learning are essential to the long-term recall of the learning material. Without them, your study material will look boring and meaningless. Motivation also affects your curiosity to learn and research more about the study content.

If you have other pressing issues that engage your mind, it is best to clear them before you start to study. Studying for an exam is beyond opening the book and turning the pages. You need to fully concentrate to easily retain the information.

Take regular breaks during studies

You have a goal, and studying smart is the name of the game. However, taking regular breaks during studies will make you more productive. The breaks will help your brain absorb more information, as concentration tends to impair after one and a half to two hours of continuous study.

> *"Having the initial study and subsequent review or practice be spaced out over time generally leads to superior learning than having the repetition(s) occur in close temporal succession (with total study time kept equal in both cases). This phenomenon is called the spacing effect (sometimes also referred to as the benefit of distributed practice)."* **—Sean H. K. Kang, Dartmouth College, Hanover, NH, USA (2016)**

The above quote confirms that for a study to be useful, one must allow enough time between two study periods. For long study hours, you can still remember some information, but the effectiveness diminishes as you study longer.

In fact, some people complain that they become stressed and sometimes forget what they have learned after long hours of study.

Therefore, it makes no sense studying all day or night long. Adequate rest and sleeping can increase your concentration span and understanding of the study material.

Don't let distractions destroy your attention

There are many sources of distraction that can steal your attention and make you misplace priorities during studies. This can be a call from a friend, a noisy study location, curiosity about what is trending on social media, or watching your favourite show.

If Manchester United (a well-known UK football team) fail to score, or your favourite contestant dropped out of a reality show, I know you care, and these activities are part of your life. However, you need to manage all distractions you can control, particularly during your studies. You need a 100% focus on your studies.

You can manage distraction by putting your phone on silent mode or leave it somewhere far away, e.g., keep it in your bag when you go into your study room. Do not use social media and social messengers while studying. Please switch off the TV.

If you must use the internet for reference purposes, there are system applications that can block social media or other sites to avoid distraction.

It is important you also maintain a clean desk while studying. Put away any magazines, books, or material you do not need during the studies. The materials in your surrounding can distract your mind.

In the end, all I am saying is to prioritise the limited time based on your long-term goals. Which one will you regret more? Missing a few TV shows or failing the exam? That is the route to your long-term goal.

Do not multitask during your studies

According to neuroscientists, the human brain has a limited cognitive bandwidth, that is, the working memory capacity at any given time.

Neuroscientists Daniel Levitin of McGill University, Adam Gazzaley of the University of California, San Francisco, and other experts agree that multitasking can drain our cognitive reserves.

In effect, your ability to understand study material will depend on how well you focus on the material at that point. Do not try to study and cook or chat with others at the same time. In such multitasking activities, your brain has to start to reconfigure the last activity each time you move between these tasks. It is less productive; therefore, single-tasking is the way to study.

Study timetables and self-discipline can help you FOCUS; Follow One Course Until Success.

Learn to say NO to yourself

Your friends may ask you to go to the cinema or on an outing, but you are preparing for an exam paper in a few days' time. You must learn to say no to them and move on with your plan. You won't be able to study or revise when you constantly go to the cinema or want to go to every event in town.

In some situations, you'll need to say no to yourself and your loved ones. The exam date will certainly not be extended, but there can be other days to hang out with your friends.

Frequently test yourself

Many research findings have concluded that taking a memory does test not only assesses what one knows, but also enhances later retention. This phenomenon is called the *Testing Effect*.

The *Testing Effect* is a well-established psychological effect that the act of testing someone's memory will strengthen their long-term memory. It shows the ability to retrieve valuable information when we need it.

Perform frequent knowledge tests as you read or revise your notes. Self-testing will help confirm your understanding of the subject, particularly if the test is based on past exam questions and under conditions similar to the real exam.

Remember: "Practice makes improvement."

Early to start, early to finish

Most professional bodies conduct exams in June and December every year, and this makes some students believe that they have 6 months to read their courses. Some programmes even hold exams on a quarterly basis.

However, the number of available months to read your text is between three and four if the body conducts exams every six months.

Let's imagine that you sat for an exam in the first week of June, and the next exam is likely to be the first week of December. Some students also tend to go for a break in the month of the exam, in this case, June.

Furthermore, it is recommended that you finish the syllabus at least four weeks prior to the exam. Therefore, you only have July to October (4 months) to complete the syllabus. November should be used to consolidate your knowledge through revision, and December is the exam.

You can increase your chance of exam success if you think and act like Usain Bolt, the Jamaican sprinter and the fastest man in the world. He consistently runs at high speed from the beginning to the end of a race. He doesn't hope to win during the last seconds of the race, and you too should not expect to pass during the last minute of the semester.

If you decided to take a course, you should start to read and practise your notes early.

When I was in high school, I consistently read and practised my notes from day one of each term until the final exam paper. In fact, I was known to be ahead of the class in many subjects. This habit led to excellent results for me.

Three things can happen to students who do not start their study early:

- Incomplete coverage of the course syllabus

- Not enough time to revise and practise for the exam

- Last-minute reading and revision, which can lead to intense pressure and stress

Any of the above three can make you fail the exams. If you start to read and practise your notes early, it will help you finish the syllabus and be able to start revising for the exams.

Your chances of passing any exam will be higher with 3 hours' daily study for 30 days than with 15 hours' daily study for 5 days.

Divide and rule

Once you determine the number of modules to study, you should divide up the subjects based on the level of difficulty. Subjects or modules that require more time to understand should be given higher priorities during studies.

You should also divide each subject into sections or topics. Set a time for when you will finish reading each section. If you are doing a calculation subject, set a time goal for the solution of each problem.

This does not mean that you should abandon the easy subjects or topics. They also require study and practice. Let me share a personal story on the issue of ignoring easy subjects.

During my final year in the high school, a colleague and I decided not to study one of the subjects, Agriculture. We felt that it was an easy subject, and, after all, we were all born and raised as farmers. Guess what? We got it all wrong. We had grade A in the difficult subjects like Mathematics and Science and a B in the easy Agriculture.

Do not underrate any module or subject. All the modules or papers are essential for your professional success.

Eat well-balanced meals and get regular exercise

Three American professors studied about 9,700 schools for five academic years. They discovered that in the years when the school contracted with a healthy lunch company, students at the school scored better in the end-of-year academic tests. This confirms the importance of nutritional quality in improving student learning.

No matter the busy study and lecture schedules, you must take some time for healthy meals and exercise. Healthy eating and regular exercise can dramatically improve your concentration, memory, and energy levels. Regular exercise is also known to reduce tension and anxiety. This can be helpful in managing exam fever.

Learn the assumed knowledge

Like the academic system, the exams at higher professional levels usually assume that you have prior knowledge of the subject. For instance, it is tough to pass CFA level 2 if you have no prior knowledge of the material in CFA level 1. The same goes for ACCA advanced auditing (P7) without prior knowledge of ACCA auditing (F8).

Learning the assumed knowledge is very important if you have an exemption to the foundation level of the professional course. So, if the need arises, do not hesitate to go back a bit and study some topics of the lower level course.

You should always learn to understand, as cramming study notes for one exam can disappoint you when assumed knowledge is tested at the higher level.

Avoid question spotting

Students who are unprepared for exam sometimes want to study their notes through question spotting. However, it is impossible to question spot for professional exam papers. You need a full understanding of the syllabus according to the guidelines. My advice is to go through the entire course and do not just focus on what you think will be examined.

Assemble a Student Mastermind Group

What is a Mastermind Group?

Napoleon Hill first wrote about mastermind groups in 1937 in his evergreen book *Think and Grow Rich*. And until today, some of the world's most successful students, executives, and professionals have used it through their way to success.

Napoleon Hill defined *Mastermind* as "Coordination of knowledge and effort, in a spirit of harmony, between two or more people, for the attainment of a definite purpose."

One of the most compelling benefits of such a group is gaining the cooperation of a group of individuals who are willing to advise and share in the spirit of achieving a defined goal.

Students can also benefit from the mastermind group through a study group.

Students can call it a study group

For most students, studying means to read textbooks and notes, and practise exercises all alone. However, do you know that discussing and teaching what you've learned to someone else is one of the most powerful memory techniques? It helps you recall and retain what you teach more than just silently reading your textbooks and notes. In other words, the more you lecture others, the more you will understand the subject. It is like happiness; the best way to get it is by giving it to others.

So imagine forming a group of three to six people who come together every week for the purpose of brainstorming and encouraging each other about their studies. This could be sharing problem-solving techniques, views on case studies or discussing a particular subject. It is similar to the concept of a mastermind group, but students call it a *study group*.

Every professional course student should consider joining a mastermind group for other benefits that are in addition to passing the exams. It is an opportunity for networking, which could lead to new sales or even a potential job.

While preparing for my final ACCA papers, two banks offered me a job without me applying for them. That was through my study group contacts (the mastermind) who recommended me to their employers.

Let's get back to the group study strategies.

Group studies will help you reinforce what you know, and find out what you don't know. Being a self-study learner most of my life, I found that group study is always a win-win strategy for me. I am good at numbers, so I mostly took the lead on the numeracy topics, while I would listen to others on the reading papers.

Group studies can create an opportunity for members to share their experiences and knowledge even beyond the textbooks. This can support your understanding of a particular topic and concept. It happened to me when I was studying marketing as part of my MBA course.

Within our team, we had the marketing manager of a well-known retail brand based in Nigeria, who explained the concepts of marketing research using her experience.

When two or more people come together, there is always a need to understand the principle of the team objective. Let's discuss how to go about setting up your own group study.

How to start a study group

Start it by getting audiences or team members. It may be that you are not the only person doing the professional course in your office or community. So, make a group of three to six people to share your understanding of a particular subject or topic. You should avoid larger groups, as they are synonymous with confusion, complex decision-making, and possibly group conflict. Here are few tips for starting a study group:

1. Do not limit the membership to your friends only. I always encourage people outside my friendship network to avoid too much socialisation during the meetings. Members of different

backgrounds can create various perspectives of the subject. This can help understanding of the subject.

2. Agree on the time, day, and location of the meetings, e.g., every Saturday 10 a.m. at the MDI Complex or the Skype Platform.

3. As mentioned earlier, do not have more than 3-6 members.

4. Agree on the subject and topic ahead of the meeting.

5. Share responsibilities, such as moderators who lead the discussion on each topic during the meetings. This role should be rotated to maintain balance within the group.

6. Agree on some ground rules and guidelines, e.g., all mobiles should be silenced during the discussions, everyone must actively take part in the group activities, attendance of group meetings.

You can agree on these ground rules during the first session or when a new member joins the group.

In addition to the face-to-face study groups, there are many online forums and communities where students discuss tips, concerns, ideas, and perspectives on subjects. Check out a quality online forum for your course, and join it.

For instance, you can create a closed group on Facebook, WhatsApp, Skype, Google Hangout, and many other platforms. With modern technological development, the mastermind and study group have no boundaries. This is another key reason why I still maintain my social media accounts.

I started writing this book about two years ago, but you will be surprised to learn that 90% of the writing was done in 90 days. For the past year and a half, I was confused about the publishing platforms and better ways of writing books. I joined a mastermind community group on Facebook founded by the bestselling author Chandler Bolt. In this group, I met many first-time writers and some experienced authors.

They shared everything I needed to write a book as quickly as possible.

I guess you may be asking yourself, what if there is no suitable offline or online study group. Then create one, and invite other like-minded people to join you. You should be able to get contacts of many people via Facebook, LinkedIn, or Twitter. Check people in your community, social functions, churches, and mosques. You start the groundwork and explain the objectives of the group to them. You will be surprised how many more people are struggling with their studies than you thought.

Accountability partners (AP)

With AP, you agree with another person to share goals and support each other toward the goals.

You first share personal goals, e.g. to complete the textbook reading by the next two months. Then on a periodic basis, say weekly, you provide detailed status updates to each other.

The aim is to hold each other accountable for deadlines and outputs. While mastermind and

AP are not prerequisite to each other, they can be powerful when practised together.

Let's assume that you want to meet every Saturday through the study group, and each one of you is supposed to present one topic. The accountability session could be your first discussion about the status of your presentation, coverage of the syllabus, assignments, etc.

The idea of accountability partner works, because when people know that they are accountable to someone for results, they are motivated to work towards the goal. If you have no AP in the mastermind group, then think of your siblings, partners, or even friends. While it may be helpful for the AP to be a student, they do not necessarily have to study the same course. You just need their time and feedback on your progress report.

How about no study group and AP?

If you have no one who will listen to your lectures or join your team, then why not teach the tables, chairs, and sofas in your room. Assume that they are people listening to your speech as a subject expert.

In this case, you will not enjoy the benefits of group studies. However, the teaching will help you to recall quickly. Of course, you should only practise this behind closed doors.

I must warn you that group studies can sometimes be ineffective. You need to balance the time spent with the group and studying on your own. If the group is not productive, then think of another strategy.

Above all, sharing study notes and experience with others helps you benefit from other people's perspectives. You can cover more of the course in depth with a group than an individual can do on their own. Nonetheless, most successful students combine both methods - collaborative and personal learning styles.

In his bestselling book, *17 Secrets of Higher Flying Students,* Fela Durotoye says:

> *"It is not what you do occasionally that matters but rather the things you do consistently that produce your habits and results."*

Study consistently, and you will see success in your exams.

Success tips for revision

- Consider blocking time in your study plan for specific questions or mock exams to ensure you cover everything.

- Don't be afraid to attempt questions you have already done – especially the ones you found tricky the first time around.

- It is really important that you do some questions in full, to exam time – time management is often an issue, and the more you prepare yourself, the better you will perform in the exam.

- To keep motivation high, break some questions into individual parts, write plans or notes for some parts and do others in full.

- Work through the answers carefully – pay attention to areas you got wrong and understand where you went wrong. It is better to do a few questions well than lots of questions poorly.

- Try not to look at the answers before really attempting the questions – you won't be able to do this in the real exam!

- Do not forget to review the marking guide too – you need to understand how marks are allocated to ensure you know how to maximize them.

- Review the examining team's guidance again in the context of what you have learned.

- Remind yourself of areas that students often struggle with, and obtain tips on how to ensure you do not make the same mistakes by reviewing the examiner's reports from the last four sittings.

Source: www.accaglobal.com

Summary and action plans

Nothing can help you pass any examination if you do not study the notes and textbooks. To achieve that, you must do it religiously with focused attention and self-discipline. It is even better if you do it through a mastermind study group.

Here are a few action points from this chapter.

- List all the subjects or papers you will study for the semester

- Confirm the examination date of each paper or course

- Set a target date for completing the course textbook or syllabus

- Assess your current situation, i.e., work schedules, other commitments

- Determine your prior knowledge or strength of each paper

- Prepare a personal study timetable

- Identify an appropriate study location

- Check for any suitable study group – online or offline

Apart from studying the textbooks and notes, you can master many exam tricks and strategies using past examination questions. This takes us to our next chapter.

CHAPTER 9

PRACTISE PAST EXAM QUESTIONS

The famous author Elbert Hubbard was once asked how one became a writer. He replied, *"The only way to learn to write is to write and write and write and write and write and write and write."*

Likewise, to learn the art of passing exams, the only way to pass is to practise and practise and practise and practise and practise and practise and practise.

Have you ever heard of a successful athlete, film star, speaker, or musician who showed up for an event without practising? All these professionals know that to succeed in their career, they have to allocate some time to learn, practise and perform.

In addition to the study notes, official textbooks, and expert articles, past exam questions can significantly aid your understanding of the course material.

Catherine Coleman, an ACCA Gold medallist and P5 prize winner, said, "At first I found professional paper questions quite random and therefore difficult to prepare for, but question practice really helped me see the style of the examiner."

This chapter explains the importance and some cautionary measures on the use of past exam questions and answers.

Monitor your progress through tests

There is no better way to get ready for any exam than attempting past exam papers. You should, therefore, practise real exam papers and be your own examiner. If possible, consider taking the last ten past papers and solve them as different mock exams.

It will be helpful if you attempt these mock exams within the rules of a real exam. Assume that you are in an exam hall and observe the strict time limit of the actual exam hall. Please, no breaks to stretch your legs or eat some snacks - that will be cheating.

It can also be tempting to look at the answer when faced with a tricky question and tell yourself that you would have worked it out eventually anyway. It is an unfair and cheating practice. You have to observe the exam rules even if no one is invigilating you.

Past papers can help you understand the exam structure, the key concepts of the syllabus, and the examiner's approach. They reveal the key exam areas of the paper. If your professional qualification does not produce past questions, then practise the samples from the question bank from the approved content providers.

Reviewing the answers to past questions also gives you the opportunity to understand how to answer future exam questions. You can compare your answers to the model answers. If it is possible, you can ask another person to read your answers and give you feedback.

Another benefit of a serious mock exam is the ability to practise handwriting. Many students now use keyboards to write notes or letters. This lack of practising handwriting makes it difficult for some students to continuously write beyond 2 hours in an exam.

Whether you marked the mock examination yourself or asked another person to do it, feedback is only the first part. You must be prepared to review the areas of weakness and work on them.

Be careful of syllabus changes

In today's world, professional bodies keep on introducing new curriculums just to keep up with the rapid pace of change in their environment. This means that some of the old course textbooks and answers can be outdated due to the syllabus changes. The risk of learning with an old solution can be eliminated by using the updated version of course textbooks and revision kits.

You should exercise caution when using the 2010 past questions for an exam in 2017. For instance, tax laws and rates can vary annually while best practices and governance codes usually last for an extended period of time.

New areas may be added to the syllabus, or some outdated concept may be removed. The new section added may have no questions in the past papers, but that does not mean they are not relevant. In fact, they should be some of the topics that require a good understanding.

Predict carefully

Most students and schools look at the previous questions and try to predict the examinable areas for the session. This is very risky, and you can miss out.

I have practised it on several occasions but never had 100% accuracy. I would list the topics in the last 10 to 15 past exams and check for any areas of concentration. If a topic has been questioned in 12 out of 15 exam sessions, it confirms that the topic is relevant for the course.

This does not mean that the other areas are not important and should be abandoned. You need to understand every area of the syllabus based on the guidelines.

However, as George Orwell wrote in his book, *Animal Farm*, "All animals are equal, but some animals are more equal than others." Every professional paper or module tends to have some important areas of focus.

In May 2017, I lectured a revision class on corporate governance to a group of MBA students. Upon review of the past questions, one of the students observed a trend of repeated questions by the examiner. Guess what? The examiner never examined any of the expected areas. Everyone was happy that we had covered the whole syllabus during revision.

Listen to successful professionals

Who better to ask about exam preparation than people who have completed the professional qualifications? They can tell you what strategies worked for them during their studies.

If you read the introduction, one of the reasons stated for writing this book is to share my own tips and strategies. You can also check with other people either offline or online; nicely ask them for some advice.

Nonetheless, I have gathered some feedback from professionals through a personal survey or an interview they had with magazines.

The individuals quoted below offer advice to students who are preparing for an exam:

Gerald Ratigan, CMA, CPA, Keynote Speaker and Bestselling Author.: "Obtaining a passing grade on a professional exam is attainable. However, it requires you to implement a Study Success Blueprint. This blueprint includes having a set study calendar that you are disciplined to follow and prioritise. Second, is to gain the confidence in yourself, which can only be obtained after arduous practising of test questions."

Samuel Grimmer ACCA and prize winner ACCA F5: "Allow yourself enough time to study and study regularly. The earlier you start to build your understanding of major topics, the more confident you will feel – you can then refine your knowledge nearer to the exam."

Joseph Owolabi, FCCA, CISA, CIA: "Success comes to those who don't quit. Make up your mind to always stay in the 'game' no matter the disappointments/failures."

Sainey Ceesay FCCA, CPFA, CISA: "Remember the age-old saying that if you want peace, you prepare for war. So the art of succeeding in any professional examination is sustained practice for examination standard scenarios. Time is of the essence here! "

Omar Fatty CAT, ACCA, CPA: "My best advice to students preparing for a professional exam is first to be committed. Prepare adequately by knowing the breadth and depth of the syllabus. Revise past exam questions sufficiently and under exam conditions. The amount of time you spend on each question should be determined by the number of marks available. Read carefully and understand all the question requirements, making sure you answer what is being asked, and not just what you want to write. Remember, credit is only given for what is relevant. Planning your answer properly and presenting it clearly, in a structured manner, is critical to getting a good score. Watch out for the quality of your answers, the strength of your arguments, as well as the structure of your presentation."

Kelepha Samba MA HRM, CIPD: "Perseverance, focus, and single-mindedness are traits one must have to successfully get through a professional course."

Assiatou Sambou LLB, BL:"Writing a professional exam has never been easy; as it is meant to prepare you for your future career. Thus, a person's intelligence alone does not guarantee a pass. It should be coupled with in-depth preparation, dedication, hard work and diligence. These guidelines if utilised wisely will lead you to make your dreams come true."

Alhagie Mbow MSc in computer information and lecturer of professional IT courses: "Know the course syllabus and key areas, get the required textbooks, form a study group with like-minded individuals whose aims are to understand the subject matter and pass the exam as well. And finally, practise, practise and practise!"

Yali Edevbie CFA "Early preparation is key, start in small chunks and read for at least 2 hours daily and build up a momentum as the exam date draws close. In addition, make use of practice questions."

Summary and action plans

Past questions can be beneficial for revision exercises. However, you need to use them with caution as question spotting can make you fail the exam. Perform the following tasks:

- Obtain the official question and answer book, if any.

- Ensure that the book is updated for the new principles, standards, law, and regulations.

- If there is no official publisher for the past questions and answers, then obtain the questions for the last 10 exam sittings usually through the website of the examination body.

- Check for any area of questions that might have changed and mark them.

PART 3

THE EXAM AND BEYOND

In the examination hall, there are three important laws of success and failure - Time, Focus, and Content.
—Ebrima Sawaneh

CHAPTER 10

THE RULES OF THE EXAM HALL

> *Time is what we want most, but what we use worst.* —**William Penn**

The above quote is true for millions of students around the world. No one should expect a good exam grade without lengthy preparation.

Time management can be categorised into two periods for the purpose of studies: Time management before the exam and during the exam. We have discussed time management tips before an exam through a careful study plan with timetables. The tips for during the exam require you to wisely use the little time allocated by the examiner.

Before the exam

Being prepared for an exam is one of the most effective means of avoiding issues. Your months of hard work and studies can be in vain if you fail to observe some important principles before entering the exam hall.

The principle of arriving on time, relaxing, and entering with the right tools can affect your working memory.

Know the exam location and time

Make sure that you know the date, start time, and location of your exams. After all, serious students have all the critical information at their fingertips.

Be there on time

Obviously, the allocated time for the exam is intended for those who started on time. Arriving late at the exam venue can lead to confusion, and it can put you under pressure as you rush to catch up with others.

You should watch out for the traffic from your residence to the exam centre. If you have not been to the venue before, ask someone like a taxi driver at least a day before the exam. You should leave very early if you are travelling by car or public transport.

I used to wake up as early as 5 am for an exam that started at 9 am. Sometimes the traffic to Lagos, Nigeria, could make you miss your exam.

I have seen students who arrived almost 30 minutes after the official starting time. They seemed confused and found it difficult to concentrate on the exam questions.

Relax very well the night before the exam

Do not spend the whole night on last-minute revision. Your brain needs to rest and get ready for the long journey of thinking and writing. Try to sleep for at least seven hours on the night before the exam.

Get all the important tools and documents

You should ensure that all the necessary tools are in place. Two or three pens; a watch to keep track of the time, a calculator, set box, etc. You would not want to imagine the pressure and stress when your only one pen fails to write in the middle of the exam.

Do not forget that some exam authorities require proof of identity with a photograph and an examination docket. Without any of the required documents, you could be delayed or denied access to the exam hall.

Avoid unnecessary discussions

When you arrive at the exam centre, it is better to sit quietly than to engage in a pointless debate. Avoid speaking with students who are not prepared, express negativity about the exam or distract your attention. For instance, some students want to discuss their views on the key areas, possible examinable topics, etc. The anxiety of other unprepared students can affect your mood.

While waiting for the exam to start, you can remain calm and become focused by listening to music, or anything that helps you feel positive.

Some important rules in the exam hall

The speed of the wall clock in the exam hall is one thing most students wish they could control. It always seems like the clock is running extra fast during the exam.

The reality is that you have several months to study but few hours to write and pass the exam. Therefore, it is important that you effectively manage the fast-moving time during the exam.

Let's discuss some techniques that will ensure efficient use of your time during exams.

Preplanning actions in the exam

Ensure you have the right question paper

If you frequently write a paper-based examination, it may have happened that you were once given the wrong question paper. To avoid this issue, it is better you first check the name and course level written on the exam paper before reading anything else.

Although you should not turn over the paper until the invigilator asks you to start, you have to ensure that the correct exam paper is on your desk.

Read the examiner's instructions

Your first action in an exam is to carefully read the examiner's instructions. How many questions are to be answered? Is there a requirement to answer a specific question?

An exam might require that you must answer question 1 and then 3 other questions. Some exams might instruct you to "answer all the questions."

Failure to answer the questions in line with the examiner's instructions can either lead to a waste of valuable time or loss of marks.

High levels of anxiety limit your working memory

According to the UK NHS, "Anxiety is a feeling of unease, such as worry or fear, that can be mild or severe." We all experience anxiety at some point in life – for example, you may feel worried and anxious about sitting an exam, or having a medical test or a job interview.

However, by worrying about your ability to pass an exam, you are reducing the working memory capacity of your brain, leaving less space for the actual exam questions in front of you. It is well-known that many students perform poorly in exams due to a high level of anxiety and stress.

Try to relax as much as possible. With the effort from your reading and practice, you will manage to answer most questions, and, hopefully, pass the exam.

However moderate anxiety can also boost academic performance, as exam fear can motivate you to study and practice. For instance, due to the fear of failure, most students are motivated to study for exams, but too much of the same fear makes them not understand the examination questions.

There are some relaxation strategies you can do right before the exam to help you stay calm. These include deep breathing in and out and / or closing your eyes and imagining the positive things in life. This positive imagination can divert your attention from failure and its consequences. Learn what works for you, and follow the same steps each time you have exams.

Do not confuse yourself

It happens that most students get confused or stressed if they are unable to respond to the first question of the exam. Do not panic; just move to the next question. Most theory or practice-based exams allow you to respond to the questions in any order. If you have the time, you can take on that particular question late.

However, if you have started a question but then decide to move on, ensure that you leave enough space before starting the next question.

Read the questions and plan the answers

Check the allocated mark for each question

Many professional examinations show the mark allocation for the part of their theory and case study-based questions. For me, this is valuable information that can help in planning the answers. It is logical for anyone to expect that a question with 10 marks requires more detailed information or analysis than a question with only 3 marks. For example, let's look at two Bar examination questions:

1. Contrast common law and civil law classes of legal system (10 marks)

2. Discuss the term judicial precedence in common law system (4 marks)

This should indicate that the examiner wants you to write more on question 1 than question 2. If I were writing this paper, I would explain four to five differences between the two legal systems and provide 2 countries as an example to each of these systems. However, for question two, I would explain the term with a simple case study and move on to the next question.

Prioritize your questions

Sometimes it is better to work on the easy questions first and then proceed to the difficult ones. If you have two short essays and one case study question in the space of three hours, you don't want to spend an hour on one difficult short question at the expense of the easy case study. Starting with the easy question would not only help get your scores, but it can also help you build more confidence about the exam. However, this method has the risk of accidentally skipping some questions.

You should not spend more time on any question than necessary, as chances are, you will end up with no time for other questions. The unanswered questions are earning you zero marks.

How can you allocate time to the question?

First, allocate the exam time according to the score for each question. Write down the estimated finishing time for each question and try not to use more time than this estimate.

If you have three hours for 100 multiple-choice questions, then 1.5 minutes can be used for each question. The remaining 30 minutes can be utilised for reviewing the answers.

Note that some computer-based examination systems do not allow for revision. Such systems usually mark your response as you submit the answers. Understanding the testing system will help you avoid this problem.

Read the questions carefully

Always carefully read the exam question before putting the mighty pen to paper. Do not read the questions as if you are surfing the internet, because some examiners understand that many students fix their minds on a certain way of the examination requirements. This makes them tweak the question in a different style and requirement. Students who fall into this trap tend to answer the question they are expecting instead of the one on the paper.

It is better to read the questions more than two times than to answer them with wrong information. This can be more tempting when the questions seem familiar to one from past questions or practice book. Often, it is not exactly the same questions; so, be careful.

If the examination offers free reading time, you should start to carefully read the questions during the planning time. This will ensure that you understand the key requirements of the questions, and also make the right choice if there are options to select.

The examiners' reports from many professional exams have indicated that failure to understand the requirements of the questions is a major reason why most candidates fail to pass the exam.

Although examinations are time-limited, rushing through the questions due to the fear of time is a recipe for getting everything wrong, and ending up failing the paper.

Let's explain this further with two sample questions:

1. Explain with examples 3 factors that could cause changes in the exchange rate of the Euro against the US dollar?

2. Explain with examples 3 factors that could the cause a fall in the exchange rate of the Euro against the US dollar?

While these questions are similar, the answers are not expected to be the same. Question 1 could be responded with an answer that relates to the rise or fall in the exchange rate of the EURO/US dollar. However, question 2's answer is expected from a decrease in exchange rates only. The interesting part is that all possible answers to question 2 could be awarded a mark in question 1 but not all question 1 answers would qualify for question 2.

This is a warning that if your planned answer to two different questions is the same, then chances are, you misread the questions rather than a mistake from the examiner. In such a situation, you should go back and reread the requirements for both questions.

It also reaffirms that failure to carefully read the questions could make you provide the wrong answers. Such a situation can lead to stress and loss of time when it is realised later in the exam. That is still better than getting home and realising that you have answered the question wrongly. Oops, don't give up; there is hope, and you should learn a lesson.

Understand the action keywords or verbs

If your exam is based on multiple-choice questions, then marking the script is of less importance. However, written and theory-based answers generally expect professional answers based on capabilities, and, indeed, an understanding of the requirements. These requirements are usually presented through the keywords. For instance, when a question requires you to define or explain a concept, the expected answer is definitely not the same as the question that asked you to list something - you are supposed to write more details in the former.

Again, a review of sample answers to past questions would reveal the meaning of these key action words in an exam question.

While not exhaustive, the table below explains some of the common keywords in exam questions.

Account for: Explain why something happens; give reasons for it

Analyse: Break into parts and examine or interpret each part or situation. How they are interrelated

Assess: Determine the strength/weakness, importance, ability

Comment on: Identify the main points and give your reactions based on logic and evidence

Compare: Examine and identify the similarities and differences

Contrast: Show the differences

Critically Evaluate: Weigh arguments for and against something, assessing the strength of the evidence on both sides

Criticize: Present problems or weakness of an action or ideas with analysis and evidence

Define: Give the exact meaning of, usually a meaning specific to the course or subject

Discuss: Consider and debate for and against an issue. Write about any conflict. Remember to conclude

Distinguish: Bring out the differences between two items, concepts, viewpoints.

Describe: Give a detailed account of how or why or the key features

Examine: Look in close detail and establish the key facts and important issues surrounding the subject. Similar to critically review

Explain: Logically make an idea or situation clear with more details and relevant facts. May also include giving a reason for something or an event

Evaluate: Assess the worth of something using the argument against or for - with evidence. Sometimes personal and expert opinion

Explore: Discuss a wide range of viewpoints

Identify: Recognize or select the key points

Illustrate: Make something clear with concrete examples or evidence. Sometimes with diagrams

Interpret: Comment and give the meaning of data or other material presented. Describe relationship, provide examples

Justify: Give evidence which supports an argument or idea; show why a conclusion was made and consider any contrary opinion

Narrate: Telling it as a story and focus on the what happened

Outline: Give only the most important points. Concentrate on the key ideas, events or features

Prove: Support with facts, theories, principles, calculations, etc.

Recommend: Advise appropriate actions to pursue

Relate: Show the connections between two or more things

State: Precisely give the main features in sentences

Summarize: Provide the most important points only. May include a conclusion

To what extent: Consider how far something is true, or contributes to a final outcome

Trace: Follow the order of stages in an event, subject, or process

Underline the key requirements

Sometimes the exam questions can have multiple requirements, or what some people call *pregnant questions*. If you do not carefully read such questions, you will possibly answer only one part of the questions.

I usually underline or highlight the key words and requirements as I go through the questions for the second or third time. This helps my understanding of the overall requirement of the questions.

If the questions asked for specific examples, or to use certain theories and models, then ensure the answers cover them. For example, if you are asked to assess a firm's competitive environment using Michael Porter's 5 forces, you should not expect any mark from the examiner if you discussed it using the PESTLE model. It may seem harsh, but it does not seem fair to other students too.

If you don't answer the question asked, the examiner cannot give the marks allocated.

One of the strategies I used to understand exam questions is to rephrase the question into a simpler version, that is, in my own words. Take a look at this Economics question.

Q. Using the Gambian economy, discuss the macroeconomic effects of a significant fall in the Gambian dalasi against US dollar, combined with a simultaneous loosening of monetary policy.

In simpler English, this question is a two-part question.

- Discuss the effect of the falling dalasi against the US dollar on the Gambian economy.

- Discuss the effect of falling interest rates (loosening of monetary policy) on the Gambian economy.

It will be helpful to deal with each part separately, before considering both together.

However, it is important that you exercise caution when using this approach. You should ensure that the key words of the question are not missing. Nonetheless, if you cannot break a complex question into a simpler version, then chances are you will not answer it correctly.

Plan your answers before you write

Never pick the mighty pen and start writing as soon as the invigilator says "Start." You should plan your answer to each question. This will make the required format of the answer clear. You can also plan for the relevant introductory paragraphs, headings, and key points.

It is important that you think about the required principles, formulas, references, and evidence that could apply to the exam question or case study.

For instance, in a professional physics exam, when solving a problem that relates to the movement of an object, it is best to first look for the principle or law that can apply to the problem. Assess if it is Newton's First, Second, or Third Law of Motion, and then relate the law to the case study.

Planning your thoughts before writing will help the quality of your answers. If the question is essay-based, it is recommended that you read all the questions and write down the key points before you start the marathon. These points will help you easily recall when it is time to write the final answers. It is especially important for the last questions as the brain starts to get exhausted.

If the question is a case study, I first read the questions two or three times before reading the case. Again, this helps me underline the key requirement of the answer within the case study.

During planning, you should note down the answers in bullet points on the question sheet. Presenting the key points of your answer logically will enhance the flow and persuasiveness of your answers.

Write and review the answers

Get right to the main point

Use your first paragraph to state your introductory and strong points. Use the rest of the essay to develop and support the main points.

Write in the context of the case study

Exam questions with case studies and scenarios always expect you to write within the context of the case study. This does not mean that you cannot bring ideas from outside of the case study. However, they should make sense to the matter at hand. Most of the case studies will be related to real-life and current problems.

If you are asked to make a recommendation, then you have to make it after considering the information given. If you assumed something outside the case study, you have to explain it or provide evidence that it is relevant to the situation.

For instance, it does not make sense to recommend a reduction of the marketing and promotional budget for a firm that is reporting low profitability due to a decline in sales volume. Such an action will slowly kill the company over time. You must defend such a point with a good reason.

Show your calculations

If the exam involves numbers, it is imperative to show your calculations and steps. Most numeracy subjects allocate marks for the correct process and steps, even if the final answer is wrong.

For example, a statistics exam that requires you to calculate a correlation coefficient may award you marks for following the right steps. Similarly, accounting papers reward marks for the steps, not just the final number.

Back your points up with theories and models

Sometimes, you just want to write a clear answer and move on. However, this does not always get you the full mark. You should back the answers up with models, theories, laws, principles, and best practices of the subject.

One sample mathematics examination question can help you understand this further.

> Exam question: In the right-angled triangle, side A is 3 cm, side B is 4 cm, and side C (which is the hypotenuse) is 6 cm. You are required to comment on the length of side C (6 marks).

Student Y's answer: Side C's length is wrong; it should be 5 cm.

Student Z's answer: The length of side C cannot be 6 cm. According to the Pythagoras' theorem; in any right-angled triangle, the square of the longest side (hypotenuse) is equal to the sum of the squares of the other two sides. It should be 5 cm.

Student Y is correct by stating the right length but what makes it right? However, Student Z sounds more confident with the backing of a mathematics theory.

If you are the examiner, which of the above answers deserve your 6 marks? I rest my case.

Similarly, in an exam, if you want to refer to a particular law or regulation, then it is best to state the name of the law and possibly the section number.

It is important to always think of the theories, principles, or whatever standard that guide the subject when responding to the essay and case-based questions.

Review your answers

Always try to allocate at least 15 minutes at the end of an exam for a thorough review of your answers. You will be surprised what you can spot during this last-minute review.

It gives you the opportunity to add more relevant points and correct a few grammar and spelling errors. Check that all the diagrams are labelled, and answers are numbered. A written note without a review is prone to many mistakes.

Sometimes even a single letter can change the meaning of the whole expression. Look at these two interesting cases:

a)   I wish you were her.

b)   I wish you were here.

The omission of the letter e in the first sentence has changed the meaning. It will put you in trouble if it is a message to your partner.

The same goes for correct punctuation.

a)   Woman, without her, man is nothing.

b)   Woman, without her man, is nothing.

The position of the commas changes the meaning of the expressions. These errors can make you lose marks in a professional English or poetry exam.

While you are writing, you could miss one letter or punctuate at the wrong place. The review gives you the opportunity to correct such simple but painful mistakes.

How about multiple-choice questions?

While some of the above strategies can be applied to multiple-choice questions, there are also some specific strategies for approaching these types of questions. The method explained below is based on Cornell University's recommendation:

A. Read the question

First, read the question and understand its requirement. Make sure you look out for qualifiers and negative words before you consider the answer. A qualifier can alter the statement and make some options incorrect. They can be found in the questions or the answer choice.

For example, consider an Economics exam paper:

When the price of basic commodities increases, the demand …

(a.) Sometimes decreases (b) never decreases (c) always decreases (d) always increases (e) none of the above

The qualifiers changed the meaning of the statement (question) and the answer choice. Words such as *always, sometimes*, and never are the qualifiers in the above example.

To beat the qualifiers, you need to know the qualifier families:

- All, most, some, none (no)

- Always, usually, sometimes, never

- Great, much, little, no

- More, equal, less

- Good, bad

- Is, is not

Like the qualifiers, the negative words can also reverse the meaning of a sentence, for instance, words like *no, not, none*, and *never*, or they can be prefixes like *il-*, as in illiquid, *un-*, as in unequal, etc.

Water is the most common illiquid substance on Earth. True or false?

If you do not pay attention to the negative word, your answer would be "True."

B. Suggest the correct answer

Try to come up with the right answer before looking at the answer choices. This can be easier for easy options and simple calculations. It helps you rule out the wrong answers. Now carefully read and consider each option. A question may have more than one correct answer, and you have to pick the best one.

C. Cross out the incorrect options

As you carefully read, cross out any options that you think are wrong. This will help you focus on the remaining choices.

D. Make your choice

Make your final selection. If you are not sure and decide to jump the question, then mark it with a sign and come back to it later. Sometimes another question may give you some clues about the challenging question you jumped.

However, you have to be sure the examination system allows you to revisit the previous question. Some computer-based tests do not allow candidates to jump questions unanswered. It means that you have only one chance to answer any question.

Summary and action plans

Apart from reading the notes, there are many unwritten rules about exams. You must understand these principles to be able to answer the exam questions correctly.

As you prepare for the next exam, take the following actions:

- Know your exam – location, date, time, tools, and documents

- Practise more past exam questions

- Learn the common exam key words for the paper

- Learn all the strategies that help present a better exam paper.

CHAPTER 11

DO NOT ANNOY THE EXAMINERS

Have you ever seen an examiner angry while marking exam scripts? No. They do not get angry by frowning, but they do not give the full mark to candidates who didn't observe some basic principles.

Your final answer may be correct, but examiner can still deny you the full point. I guess you must be thinking why. This chapter discusses some "silly" mistakes that cost many students marks.

If you avoid these mistakes, then you will make the examiner happy and award you good marks.

Let's discuss some of these mistakes:

Spelling and grammar errors

Never think that the examiners will assume what you intended to write. They mark what they can read and understand. It is therefore important that your answers are logical and readable.

While most professional exams will not penalise students for grammar and style, it is important that you spell the words correctly. Writing needs to be readable and understandable by the examiner.

As a college lecturer, I used to see fundamental spelling errors on exam papers which sometimes changed the meaning of the sentence. Examiners have many papers to read and mark within a limited time. If your paper is examiner friendly, you could attract some free marks.

Yes, some examiners award professional marks for the overall quality of the answers and for effective professional communication skills.

These free marks could make the difference between a pass and a fail.

One of my colleagues once scored 48% in one session and 49% in the same paper in the next session. The pass mark was 50%. Imagine the difference if he had got one bonus mark from the examiner.

Legible writing

Poor handwriting can often lead to losing exam marks for some students. If the marker cannot read the answer script, there is little they can do for you. This is a big loss for anyone, considering the hours of preparation and the cost of the exam.

You can improve your handwriting through frequent writing exercises. If your exam is a computer-based system, then you do not have to worry about handwriting.

Personally, I used to manage my poor handwriting by controlling the speed of my writing during the exams. I write slowly and always revise my answers to correct any obvious error.

Stay within the boundaries

No matter how well you understand the subject, /you should always write within the limits of the question. If the question requests you to list, then list and move on. Explaining the list does not give you any extra marks.

In fact, you should use the extra time to review your work. If you made assumptions that are not in the qluestion, it is important that you state them in the answer script. The examiner can probably award you a mark if they sound reasonable and are related to the question.

Use the right format

One aim of creating a professional association is for practitioners to establish standard guidelines and principles. Some professions also have standard formats for presenting information and reports.

Presenting information in the wrong format can annoy markers. Actually, they will not be annoyed, but you can lose part of the mark. For instance, in accounting, a balance sheet should present assets and capital separately.

Similarly, if a question requires you to write a letter, memo or report, then follow the standard format. At this stage, you are expected to understand the presentation format of a memorandum and letter.

A *memo* is an internal document that has a subject, the names of the author and recipient, and a date. Similarly, a *report* would have a subject, aims of the report, finding, conclusion. Sometimes you may be asked to recommend an action plan.

A *letter* is addressed to someone usually outside an organization. It should be concise and written in a formal style. The salutation and signature are both necessary.

The right format and proper standard could earn you 4 to 5 marks in an examination.

Reference the answers to the questions

Proper reference in the answers to the questions aids the markers to do their job easily. The answer to question one should be marked with the one in the answer booklet. Note that most professional exams allow you to answer the questions in any order.

Label all diagrams

All diagrams and graphics should be referenced in line with the standards of the profession. Imagine a graph without a title or a table without a heading. This makes your work look unprofessional in a professional exam.

Respond in a practical way

Professional qualifications aim to educate students with practical solutions and principles that could solve the problems of society. Therefore, you can write a strong point if your answers are very practical. It makes your work more mature and professional.

Again, practising past questions would provide a feel for this approach. You could also imagine what you would write to a customer, assuming you are a consultant and the exam question came from your client.

Summary and action plans

If you have been observant in this chapter, it would be obvious to you that I haven't said that the examiners are angry when marking the scripts. I explained that the examiners are looking for best concise content in terms of clarity, presentation, and structure.

With frequent studies and self-testing, your chance to earn professional marks is very high.

Now that we have dived into the examiner's mind, let's discuss what happens after the exams.

CHAPTER 12

WHAT TO DO AFTER THE EXAM

No professional exam should be the most important event in your life. There must be other events that will make you a happy and successful person. What I mean here is that you should not bother yourself too much with the exam results.

Think about the future and plan for the next key steps that will bring you closer to your life's goals.

If your exam does not offer you instant results, then you can perform quite a number of activities during this waiting period.

Waiting for the exam results

Many students wait for the exam results before deciding their next course of action. Well, that is not a smart approach, even if that exam is your final paper for your qualification. There are lots of productive activities you can engage in while waiting for the results.

Feeling good about the exam

If you have a good feeling about your performance in the exam, then you should start to prepare for your next papers. You can borrow or buy the textbooks and prepare study notes for your next papers. If you cannot borrow or risk the investment of buying new books, then browse the internet for the syllabus, relevant articles, and journals that relate to your next papers. You can start these activities after a week or two of relaxation.

The above strategy always helped me prepare for the next session particularly when I had access to the syllabus of the papers. Additionally, it also contributed to my early completion of the course texts, which then gave me the opportunity to take multiple mock exams before the final exam.

Not feeling good about the exam

If you are not confident in your performance, then apply the strategy above to the paper you just attempted and any other paper you plan to read in the next session. One will be a revision, and other will be a note preparation.

Final exam papers

However, if you have attempted your last exam papers, then prepare to network and apply your new knowledge while you wait for the results.

You can add some work experience through internship or community services. This can help you brush up your employability skills and build your curriculum vitae(CV) for promotion or to impress future employers. Volunteering also gives you the opportunity to meet new people and network, while you give back to society.

Whether you start to prepare for the next paper or add some work experience, you should not use the waiting period as a time to only party and forget your goals.

Remember you want to acquire the qualification for reasons which relate to your burning desire and personal goals.

When the exam results are out

Sitting an exam is like tossing a coin. There are two possible outcomes: either pass it or miss the pass mark. Whatever may be the outcome, I have some tips for you.

You have passed

First of all, congratulations!

Reward yourself

One of the major ways of repeating more success in life is the art of self-reward. You do not have to wait for someone to say congratulations. Do it first. If you are working or you have access to spare free cash, then buy yourself something or go out for a nice treat. If you have a partner, then this is another opportunity to show your love.

Rewarding yourself gives you a sense of completion, and this will reinforce your subconscious mind to even work harder in the next examination. This is true for all individual successes.

Work on the next plan

If you have a few more papers to complete, then you should continue to prepare for those exams. Make another study plan and leverage what has worked for you.

However, if that was your final exam, then you have completed the hardest part of the journey.

Depending on the profession, you may have to fulfil some requirements to become a full member. Most associations require work experience and a third-party reference in addition to the formal application. If your current job does not qualify you for the relevant work experience, consider an internship in other departments.

Let's say you have applied for a professional membership and got approval or the licence. What is next? Well done once again. This is the time to consider career growth opportunities such as career change and upgrade.

Do not just put the certificate away. Share the news about membership or licence with your manager, colleagues, and network. Depending on the qualification and your passion, you could also think about starting a business.

Whatever you decide to follow, remember, the qualification is a means to an end. So, act and apply what you have learned. This is what makes you a true professional.

You have missed the Pass Mark

It is important that you appreciate that like happiness and sadness in life, passes and failures are an inevitable part of education. Learning something new, like a professional skill, is similar to stepping outside one's comfort zone, and it is bound to carry the risk of failure.

> *Failing an exam is not the issue as it is just a signal that the exam did not work for you. The most important decision is to accept that result, and prepare yourself for the next one.*

If you were unable to pass the exam, then you have two choices to make:

1. Blame people and the situation for the poor result

2. Change your action plan until you pass the exam

Yes, when people fail their exams, it is easy and common for them to blame the lecturer, society, family, office supervisor, and even their spouse. I have heard students assume that most professional bodies need a certain number of passes at every examination sitting. Trust me, I have never seen that, and I always believe it is more of an excuse than a reality. It is easy for anyone to give a thousand reasons why they failed the exam.

I want you to always remember one important thing in life: You must accept responsibility for all your results. You can never be successful if you continue to blame others or situations for your poor results. This applies to all situations: school, office, business, relationships.

However, the best choice from the above options is number 2. You change your action plan and strategy until you pass that exam. It could be that you did not cover the syllabus, or you did not even study enough.

Nonetheless, any time you fail an examination paper, there are a few basic steps you could follow:

Think about the future

The past is a sunk cost, and you cannot recover it. Therefore, you should think about the future if you failed any exam. Focus your attention on the next exam. Do not give up.

It is also an opportunity to think about the reasons why you want to acquire the qualifications. They could motivate you to prepare for the next exam.

Analyse the possible mistakes

The first step is to examine the possible mistakes you may have made in the examination. If the examination questions and answers are available, this will help you complete this step.

Prepare a new action plan to tackle the paper

Make a new action plan for the next exam. This could range from a new study plan to different study materials to changing your learning method. I met a student who failed one exam paper. However, on joining a study group, he was able to understand the subject better and pass the exam.

If you keep on doing what you have always done, you will keep on getting what you have always got.
—Jack Canfield, Bestselling author, Success Principles

In other words, Jack is saying that if you want to see a different result, then you must change your action plan.

Start to implement these new strategies and check how you are progressing through periodic mock exams.

Remember the reason why you failed the examination. There are hundreds of candidates who have faced the same situation, and today, they have acquired their professional qualifications.

Summary and action plans

The result of every exam is either pass or fail. Sometimes you may think of giving up and walking away. However, the scores do not truly reflect your ability. It simply means that you were not prepared for that examination. If you keep pushing and devise a solid study plan, your next attempt can be successful.

"The past cannot be changed. The future is yet in your power."
—Unknown

If you completed all the exams, then start to become a true professional. Your work starts now. Join the millions of professionals and let's make the world a better place for everyone.

Good luck!

BONUS CHAPTER 13

BENEFITS OF PROFESSIONAL QUALIFICATIONS

Why make this the last chapter?

You may expect this topic to appear as the first chapter of a professional self-help book. However, the focus of this book is not why you need to acquire professional certification.

It is about the tips and strategies that can help anyone pass their professional exams.

Therefore, I want the reader to focus on the subject. This book is for those who have already learned about the importance of professional qualifications and have even made a choice of qualifications to pursue.

Nonetheless, I believe this topic will also help many new graduates or young people who are still trying to decide their career path.

Whatever profession you intend to follow, there is a possible career path and related growth strategy. Among the personal development growth strategies, acquiring a professional qualification is one of the reliable methods you will learn from mentors, career counsellors, and loved ones.

A bit about professional qualifications

When it comes to higher education, there are two broad categories: the academics and the professionals. Most people begin with academic degrees; however, you will rarely find anyone succeeds in the corporate world without some general professional training or certification.

For instance, you might read for a bachelor's degree or even a master of science degree in accounting. However, you will need professional development training in the latest accounting standards and best practices to succeed in the dynamic accounting world. Similar issues apply to the legal profession, engineering, technology, marketing, and even medicine.

Professional bodies combine a number of skill sets and values that are relevant to the practical work environment either as an employee, a consultant, or an entrepreneur. They aim to assess students' abilities to apply the set skills before awarding them membership status.

Additionally, most professional associations require continuous development from their members, and some even ask for periodic re-examination to confirm that their members are up to date with the changes affecting the profession and its stakeholders.

Note that emphasising the importance of professional qualifications is by no means implying that the academic system is not relevant to the work environment. In fact, professional skills and standards are based on the foundation of university research and reports.

Furthermore, as you will notice later in this chapter, when was the last time you received a technical, industry, or management skills update from your university or college? Only a few schools perform such roles for their alumni, and they are mostly focused on their own research or news.

On the other hand, professional bodies are built around their members and tend to provide a comprehensive range of updates.

While the tenure for most academic courses is long and requires massive commitment, professional courses help you update your knowledge within a short period of time.

Let's check some of the general benefits of professional qualifications:

Follow a career path

Your first degree could offer you a range of jobs, but a professional qualification gives you an opportunity to study a particular job function. If you want to follow a marketing career path, then a course with the Chartered Institute of Marketing (CIM) could be very relevant in addition to your bachelor of science degree in business.

If you want to be a finance executive of a major company, then professional training and experience are critical to reaching this goal.

Learn practical skills

Learning how engineers construct a bridge is a theory, but actively being involved in bridge construction for clients is a practice. This is one of the benefits of professional qualifications.

If you study a structural engineering course, you may be asked to take part in the design or supervision of a construction project as part of the membership requirements. This practice will equip you with skills that are relevant to real-life situations.

Similarly, a professional marketing course may ask you to prepare a marketing campaign for a new product instead of just learning various theories of marketing for a new product.

I have explained in Chapter 7 that many professional bodies will not award membership status even after passing all the required examinations. Successful students must undergo practical training and gather some experience before they can become full professional members.

Easy to get a job or clients

In many industries, it is easier to get a job when you acquire professional certification in addition to your university degree.

You will learn the theories in a degree programme. However, a professional certification process makes you practise some of these theories. This makes it easy for most employers to choose professional candidates, particularly those with post-qualification experience.

The word *professional* sounds nice, doesn't it? Well, whether you like it or not, customers and the industry will judge you based on this one word.

Therefore, if you want to practise as an entrepreneur or consultant on technical matters, it is better you add some professional qualifications to your CV , or you will miss many opportunities.

If you take note of the most highly paid job adverts or invitations for a bid, you may realise the requirement for applicants to be professionally qualified. Some companies include it as a 'must have' requirement while others would say that it is advantageous. The certification offers some assurance to the company that the candidate or bidder has acquired a specific set of skills and knowledge of the job.

Growth and promotion opportunities

Let's say you got a good job with a bachelor's degree. However, your progress can be hard if you do not acquire any professional training. Remember, the professionals went through competency-based exams and adhered to continuous self-development.

Employers may not tell you or include it in the official policy documents, but career growth could be affected if you have no professional qualifications for some job functions.

I received three job offers within 6 months upon completion of my ACCA level 2 in 2008. Guess what? I did not accept any of the offers, as I wanted to focus on my studies. The Gambia was short of trained professional accountants. I finished the whole ACCA qualification in 2009 and obtained membership in March 2010. In October 2010, I got another offer from the local office of an international bank, and in September 2011, I took an international job in Lagos, Nigeria.

You may start to say that my case is one in a thousand, and you may be right. However, I recommend that you check out the trained professionals in your community. They are running successful businesses or benefiting from highly paid jobs.

Update on industry information

As stated earlier, a degree is still essential. However, your professional qualifications can set you apart from the rest of the employees. Professional bodies are known to provide periodic updates on developments that could affect their members. This includes technical, regulation, and even soft skills articles. They run blogs, webinars, official newsletters, etc.

When was the last time you received an email update from your university or college? Chances are it related to the international developments and news about the school and not what you studied with them. This is partly because academic institutions focus on many career areas. One university can offer engineering, business, accounting, fashion, etc. On the other hand, professional bodies offer related courses, e.g. accounting and finance or fashion and modelling. A fashion association would not offer accounting certification.

Statutory or regulatory requirement

In many jurisdictions, you cannot practise some job functions without a valid licence from a particular body or regulator. These regulators mostly rely on professional certification to award or reject licences. For example, in the UK, you cannot sign a public financial statement as an external auditor without a licence from a professional accounting association.

The same rule applies in the United States, Nigeria, and all over the world. You also cannot offer legal advice if you are not licensed or a member of the bar. A similar issue affects engineering, doctors, financial advisers, etc. The law trusts professional associations in such a way that clients and employers want to deal with only certified people.

Whether you want to be an entrepreneur or employee, the above benefits should make you appreciate the reason why everyone is taking professional courses.

Summary and action plans

If you have not chosen any profession to pursue, then I recommend that you do a self-assessment. It starts with the why. Why do I want to acquire a professional qualification? The long-term answer to this can only be related to your passion. Many people have acquired certification they never use. One reason is that they pursued the qualification for reasons other than their passion.

ABOUT THE AUTHOR

Ebrima B Sawaneh, also known as "Mansa", is a chartered accountant, banker, blogger and Amazon International Bestselling Author.

Originally from the Gambia, Ebrima works as an accountant for a Lagos-based development financial institution. He is passionate about personal development, empowerment and education. Ebrima is always looking for an opportunity to impact the lives of other people.

He is the Founder of Business-in-Gambia (www.businessingambia.com), an educational blog where he teaches many young Africans about small business and personal finance management. He is also the President of Next Generation Foundation that provides educational support and training to young people in the Gambia.

Ebrima's expertise lies in finance, accounting, and banking. He taught these subjects at the Management Development Institute and Nusrat Management & Accountancy Training Centre for over 5 years. He also lectures Corporate Governance to MBA students on a part-time basis.

Ebrima is a Fellow of the Association of Chartered Certified Accountants (ACCA). He also holds a BSc in Applied Accounting (Hons) degree from Oxford Brookes University and an MBA in Finance from Heriot-Watt University in Edinburgh in the UK.

His other professional qualifications include Certified Accounting Technician, Certified Islamic Finance Executive (CIFE) and ISO27001 Implementer. He learned most of these courses through self-study.

Ebrima loves community service, outdoor activities, and farming. You can connect with him online at http://ebrimasawaneh.com

FEEDBACK

First , thank you for purchasing this book. I really appreciate your feedback and would love to hear what you have to say.

If you enjoyed this book, I'd like to ask you a big favour. Did this book give you some clues to pass a professional exam? In what way? What did you find useful in this book?

Please post a review for this book on Amazon.

Your feedback will help others make a more informed decision when considering whether to buy this book. It will also help me to improve the next version.

All the best,
Ebrima B Sawaneh, FCCA

GET UPDATES

"Passed" is the first in a series of books that will help many young professionals.
If you'd like to be informed when my next books will be published, let me know. I will add your name to my friendship contact list. Visit www.ebrimasawaneh.com or email me.

Do not forget to download your copy of my **gift** for you. **http://ebrimasawaneh.com/passedgift/**

How else can Ebrima help you? Kindly contact me at eb@ebrimasawaneh.com

WANT TO WRITE A BOOK?

If you want to learn how I wrote this book in 90 days, then I recommend the Self-Publishing School. The founder offers free exclusive video through the link below.

Even if you're busy, bad at writing, or don't know where to start, you CAN write a bestseller and build your best life.

https://xe172.isrefer.com/go/curcust/
bookbrosinc3227

REFERENCES AND RESOURCES

The following books and websites were either quoted or read during the preparation of this book.

Books

Canfield, Jack (2005). *The Success Principles.* HarperCollins Publishers Ltd: London

Carmine, Gallo (2014). *Talk like TED*. St. Martin's Press: New York

Durotoye, Fela (2006) *17 Secrets of High Flying Students.* Visible Impact Multimedia Group. Lagos

Ellis, D. (1998). *Becoming a Master Student*. Houghton Mifflin: Boston

Hill, Napoleon (1928). *The Law of Success.* The Ralston University Press: New York

Hill, Napoleon (1960). *Think and Grow Rich.* Random House Publishing: New York

Ringer, Robert J. (2014*). Million Dollar Habits.* Skyhorse Publishing: New York

Tracy, Brian (2002). *Create Your Own Future: How to Master the 12 Critical Factors of Unlimited Success.* John Wiley & Sons Inc: Hoboken

Websites

Kelly Wallace, CNN. *Teens spend 9 hours a day using media, report says - CNN.* [ON-LINE] Available at: http://edition.cnn.com/2015/11/03/health/teens-tweens-media-screen-use-report/.

Cindi May. *A Learning Secret: Don't Take Notes with a Laptop - Scientific American.* [ON-LINE] Available at: https://www.scientifi-camerican.com/article/a-learning-secret-don-t-take-notes-with-a-laptop/.

Halmut D. Sachs. *The SQ3R Method of Studying – The Father of All Reading Methods is Alive and Kicking • RememberEverything.*

[ONLINE] Available at: https://rememberev-erything.org/the-sq3r-method-of-studying/.

Dr. V.K. Maheshwari,*Open Book Examination – examination that tests the skills of problem solving and critical thinking,* | *Dr. V.K. Maheshwari,* [ONLINE] Available at: http://www.vkmaheshwari.com/WP/?p=2259.

John Wihbey. *Cognitive control in media multitaskers - Journalist's Resource.* [ONLINE] Available at: http://journalistsresource.org/studies/society/internet/cognitive-control-in-media-multitaskers.

Andrea Leyden. *Student life: 10 study tips to improve your revision - Telegraph.* [ONLINE] Available at: http://www.telegraph.co.uk/education/universityeducation/student-life/10784360/Student-life-10-study-tips-to-improve-your-revision.html?-frame=2891351

CFA. *CFA Exam Topic Area Weights.* [ONLINE] Available at: https://www.cfainstitute.org/programs/cfaprogram/exams/Pages/exam_topic_area_weights.aspx

ACCA - http://www.accaglobal.com. 2017. *Study Skills | ACCA Global.* [ONLINE] Available at: http://www.accaglobal.com/gb/en/student/sa/study-skills.html.

University of Leicester. *Essay terms explained — University of Leicester*. [ONLINE] Available at: http://www2.le.ac.uk/offices/ld/resources/writing/writing-resources/essay-terms.

University of Reading. *Effective note-making -Reading and making notes - University of Reading*. [ONLINE] Available at: http://libguides.reading.ac.uk/reading/notemaking

Michael L. Anderson, Justin Gallagher, and Elizabeth Ramirez Ritchie. *How the quality of school lunch affects students' academic performance*. [ONLINE] Available at: https://www.brookings.edu/blog/brown-center-chalkboard/2017/05/03/how-the-quality-of-school-lunch-affects-students-academic-performance/

Learning Strategies Center. *The Cornell Note-taking System | Learning Strategies Center*. [ONLINE] Available at: http://lsc.cornell.edu/study-skills/cornell-note-taking-system/.

Corinne Purtill. *The scientific case for single-tasking instead of multitasking — Quartz*. [ONLINE] Available at: https://qz.com/976473/the-scientific-case-for-single-tasking-instead-of-multitasking/.

ACCA. *Pass rates for ACCA qualifications | ACCA Global*. [ONLINE] Available at: http://www.accaglobal.com/pk/en/student/exam-support-resources/pass-rates-for-acca-qualifications.html.

The Common Sense Census. *The Common Sense Census: Media Use by Tweens and Teens | Common Sense Media*. [ONLINE] Available at: https://www.commonsensemedia.org/research/the-common-sense-census-media-use-by-tweens-and-teens.

Duckworth, Angela & Seligman, Martin. (2006). Self-Discipline Outdoes IQ in Predicting Academic Performance of Adolescents. Psychological science. 16. 939-44. 10.1111/j.1467-9280.2005.01641.x.

Sarah green. *The Right Mindset for Success*. [ONLINE] Available at: https://hbr.org/2012/01/the-right-mindset-for-success.

ACCA. *Prizewinning exam advice | Student Accountant | Students | ACCA Global*. [ONLINE] Available at: http://www.accaglobal.com/gb/en/student/sa/study-skills/dec2014-prizewinners.html

CIPD. *How to Prepare for Exams | Study Guide | CIPD*. [ONLINE] Available at: https://www.cipd.co.uk/knowledge/students/study-guides/exam-prep

Open University. *After the examination - Skills for OU Study - Open University*. [ONLINE] Available at: http://www2.open.ac.uk/students/skillsforstudy/after-the-examination.php.

Michael C. Friedman. Notes on Note-Taking: Review of Research and Insights for Students and Instructors- Harvard University. [ONLINE] Available at: http://hilt.harvard.edu/files/hilt/files/notetaking_0.pdf

Jennifer Mishra. Content-Dependent Memory: Implications for Musical Performance. University Houston. [ONLINE] Available at: www.uh.edu/~tkoozin/cognition/Mishra+CDM+Update.pdf

Sean H. K. Kang. Spaced Repetition Promotes Efficient and Effective Learning: Policy Implications for Instruction. Dartmouth College. [ONLINE] Available at: https://www.dartmouth.edu/~cogedlab/pubs/Kang(2016,PIBBS).pdf

Success Values www.successvalues.com

CFA Institute www.cfainstitute.org

ACCA Global www.accaglobal.com

IPassTheCPAExam www.iPassTheCPAExam.com

Good Read www.goodreads.com

Brainy Quote https://www.brainyquote.com

REVIEWS

"**PASSED** is a great book full of practical tips and guidelines that will help academic and professional students prepare and pass their examination.

Ebrima Sawaneh explicitly gives an account of his secrets (and probably my own secrets) and approach to passing the ACCA.

I love the summary and action plan at the end of each chapter, especially his "How to read textbooks and prepare study notes". This chapter is fantastic!

The author also shares some personal stories which will inspire many young Africans that, with determination, hard work and perseverance, there is no limit to what one can achieve.

I recommend this best-selling book to all students, particularly African students who think that humble beginnings constrain their growth in life."

—Omar Mboob, FCCA,
Head, Corporate Banking,
Trust Bank Limited Banjul, The Gambia

———

'Ebrima Sawaneh's **PASSED** chronicles practical steps (secrets) to pass professional examinations in the first attempt.

The book steps out of the traditional approach and presents itself in the most personal way for readers to relate to their own examination journey. Alongside accounts from established professionals and practitioners, the book offers an accessible personal account of proven steps on how one can pass professional examinations with ease.

It is, therefore, a book I can recommend without reservation.

—Alieu K Jarju,
Director General, Management Development Institute (MDI) Kanifing, The Gambia

———

"This book is a terrific and fabulous piece. Every page offers something amazing. Ebrima is the best penman to write on this subject as I have watched him rise from obscurity to prominence. Once you begin reading the book, it is unputdownable!

PASSED is a must-have for everyone who desires outstanding success in any professional examination."

—Desmond Onyemechi Okocha,
MA, PhD, Founder/Executive Director, Institute for Leadership and Development Communication, Abuja, Nigeria

————

Compressed and on point. Easy to read and understand as Sawaneh's proven practical steps and guidelines are precise, which is very important when you are getting ready for an examination.

—Amie Njie Sowe,
AAT Student Member, Birmingham, United Kingdom

————

"**PASSED** draws many inspirational lessons for readers to learn from or be inspired by reading all the chapters in the book. It explores the tough and difficult journey of the writer and explains in vivid terms how he was able to stand the "test of time" and prove himself in the world full of challenges, and of which the poor are always at a disadvantage.

In short, the book distinguishes itself by wading into issues which many professionals often ignored or felt unwilling to share.

I wish to offer my gratitude to the author for sharing his story with such a captivating tome."

—**Assan Jallow,** PhD,
ChE Senior Compliance Strategist,
Gambia Revenue Authority,
Banjul, The Gambia

———

With **PASSED**, Ebrima has given us a book that epitomizes a practical philosophy to not just taking professional exams, but to learning and proper application of knowledge. It has a universal applicability to preparing for any examination, but it is also loaded with eternal wisdom packaged in utter simplicity.

This masterpiece is delivered in a crisp and concise style to give the reader everything he/she needs in preparing for professional exams with mathematical exactitude, and a lot more to use in life.

—Jamal Drammeh,
Author of **Life Balance & Abundance**
Business Consultant, USA

———

"Ebrima Sawaneh's book inspired me when I was preparing for my postgraduate exams. It has taught me how to focus on my studies among many other things."

—Assan N Sanyang,
Postgraduate in Management (ICM),
Medical Research Council (MRC)Unit,
Fajara, The Gambia

———

30608456R00133

Made in the USA
San Bernardino, CA
28 March 2019